Folksies,

Many, many tha[nks] [   ] [   ] [   ] [   ] ere
ver[s]ary present [   ] [   ] [   ]
[   ] [   ] [   ] early. As it ha[d]
[   ] d[i]n't get anything yet. If the[y]
[   ] furnish a long mirror for
[   ] use the $10 on a copper fra[me]
[   ]sen mirror — so we looked
[we] have to wait + see. Wouldn'[t]
[   ]ning? That would be a re[al]
[w]e are both thrilled to have
[   ]hal!

[   ] Before I forget, Mrs Hugh
[Chr]istine) whose husband is [   ]
[C]oolidge, is going back to Ne[w]
[   ]l you if she goes thru Colum[bus]
[i]t grand + I know you'd e[   ]
[Hu]gh + Chris are always so nic[e]
[whe]n she mentioned going bac[k]
[you]'d like to meet you

[   ] Well, it just seems imp[   ]
[w]e've done lately. The trip to C[   ]

Letters from Wupatki

Courtney Reeder Jones

Edited by Lisa Rappoport

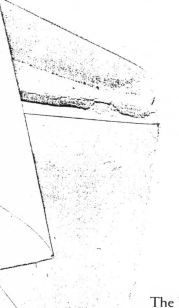

The University of Arizona Press Tucson

The University of Arizona Press
Printed in the United States of America

♾ This book is printed on acid-free, archival-quality paper.
00 99 98 97 96 95   6 5 4 3 2 1
Library of Congress Cataloging-in-Publication Data
Jones, Courtney Reeder, 1915–
    Letters from Wupatki / Courtney Reeder Jones ; edited by Lisa B. Rappoport.
    p. cm.
    Includes bibliographical references.
    ISBN 0-8165-1530-1 (alk. paper). —
    ISBN 0-8165-1507-7 (pbk. : alk. paper)
    1. Wupatki National Monument (Ariz.) 2. Jones, Courtney Reeder, 1915–
    —Correspondence. 3. Navajo Indians. 4. Pueblo Indians—Antiquities.
5. Arizona—Antiquities. I. Rappoport, Lisa B., 1953–   II. Title.
E78.A7J67 1995   94-18756
979.1'33—dc20   CIP

British Cataloguing-in-Publication Data
A catalogue record for this book is available from the British Library.

In memory of David J. Jones

Contents

List of Illustrations   ix

Editor's Preface   xi

Acknowledgments   xv

Introduction:
The Magic of Reality   xvii

Letters from Wupatki   3

Afterword   143

Notes   147

Illustrations

Wupatki from the north and the east   4

Courtney and Davy at their wedding,
   April 20, 1938   7

Wupatki from the northwest   9

Betatakin Ruin, Navajo National Monument   11

Sally Peshlakai weaving   13

Courtney in the ruin pantry   16

Courtney in the ruin kitchen   19

Courtney and Davy in the ruin   23

Frank Pinkley, Ruth Egermeyer, and Natt Dodge   24

Courtney, Charley Clyde, and Sally Peshlakai   26

Courtney throwing out the dishwater   27

Picnic on a trip to Moenkopi, 1938   31

Davy putting a roof on the refrigerator room   35

Davy and Courtney climbing the ladder to their
   apartment   37

Courtney showering   44

Sally Peshlakai   48

Clyde Peshlakai   50

Catherine Peshlakai and her children outside a
   hogan   53

The new house at Wupatki   64

Wukoki ruin   66

Catherine and Sally Peshlakai shearing sheep   68

Courtney and her father, George Reeder   71

Courtney and Davy at the mailbox   84

Picnic at the mailbox   85

Charley Clyde Peshlakai   87

Nez ka Yazzie, the medicine man, and a
   sandpainting   94

Sally and Catherine Peshlakai fixing their niece's
   hair   104

Sallie Brewer   106

Courtney and Modesta Dixon   124

Clyde Peshlakai and Mady Fleming   130

Courtney, Janie, and Davy Jones, Christmas 1947
   134

Janie Jones and Ray Peshlakai   137

Janie Jones wearing a Navajo dress   139

Courtney, Davy, and Janie in her moccasins   140

Courtney at Wupatki, 1988   144

Editor's Preface

I met Courtney and Davy Jones in Santa Fe in 1981. Davy and I used to see each other walking our dogs around the neighborhood, and one day I mentioned the courteous gentleman with the handsome black collie to my friend Litzi. "Oh, that must be Davy Jones, he and his wife Corky live near you. They're wonderful," she said.

Several years after we met, Courtney mentioned that her sister Edna was typing up the letters Courtney had written between 1938 and 1949, when she and Davy (who worked for the National Park Service) had lived at Wupatki National Monument north of Flagstaff, Arizona. "Someone should make these into a book," I said after reading them, and that was the beginning of our collaboration. I was not only a friend but also a writer and photographer, and I began editing and annotating the letters, collecting vintage photographs, and making copy negatives to print for the book.

The trips I made to Wupatki in Courtney's company, and our visits with Sally Peshlakai Lee, her frequent companion when they lived there, are treasured memories. Inez Paddock, Sally's cousin who works for the Park Service, was our translator, guide, and liaison.

These letters, which fall into two groups, were selected from 180 that were saved by Courtney's family and her friend "M." (who wishes to remain anonymous). The first

are those written to the Reeder family in Nebraska. Courtney's parents, George and Hazel Perrin Reeder, and her
twin sisters Edna ("Liz") and Marian lived next door to
George's parents, Grandfather Reeder (who died in 1938)
and George's mother Lillian ("Gagoo"). Aunt Clara Reeder,
George's older sister, lived at home to help care for her
mother, who was crippled by arthritis. Courtney's parents
moved from Columbus, Nebraska, to Berkeley and Los
Gatos, California, during World War II, and then to Hollis-
ter, Missouri.

Both of Courtney's grandmothers were pioneers. Grandmother Perrin ("Ganga") lived in a sod house and taught
school in western Nebraska, and Gagoo was raised at a
trading post on Nebraska's Loup River. Ganga spent three
years in Tucson, Arizona, for her health before returning to
Lincoln in 1940.

The second group of letters went to M., a friend from
the 1936 University of Arizona archaeological expedition
where Courtney and Davy met. (They met Mary Jane and
Tad Nichols on that trip as well.) M. lived part of the time
on a ranch outside Tucson but moved around the country
frequently. The tone of the letters to M. is a little more
open. Courtney said that when writing to her family, she
naturally tried to present things in a good light because she
didn't want them to worry about her, whereas with M. she
was somewhat freer in mentioning the more difficult as-
pects of her life.

About fifty letters were omitted entirely, including many
of those written during the war years. Although Courtney's
account of living in the United States at that time is fascinating, the Joneses were away from Wupatki for three
years; that period belongs to another story. I also omitted
many passages that gave more information about the relatives in Nebraska than about Wupatki. My aim was to

select letters that best convey the quality of Courtney's daily life in this unique situation.

One of the no longer used adjectives of these letters, and those years, is "rare." This word aptly describes the author of these letters, and her way of experiencing the world, even when faced with tragedy.

Courtney and Davy's daughter Sal disappeared at sea in 1979 while sailing with her husband Agamemnon off the coast of northern Africa. After the long silence, the Joneses decided to travel up and down the coast with photographs of Sal and Ag, asking in each village for news of the lost couple or the boat. Despite the pain of losing a child, Courtney spoke of this trip as another adventure. She and Davy somehow found a way to take pleasure in the voyage, while in no way diminishing its grief. This seemed to me a powerful lesson, an example of how to embrace life, even while enduring a great loss.

Courtney's rare ability to embrace life is evident throughout the letters she wrote from Wupatki. I hope readers will find this glimpse of her life as vivid and compelling as I did.

Lisa Rappoport

Acknowledgments

I would like to first thank Courtney Reeder Jones's sister Edna Reeder Emerson (aka "Lizzie Begay/Liz the Whiz") for taking on the indispensable hard work of collecting, typing, and dating Courtney's letters, copies of which have been donated to the Museum of Northern Arizona. The staff at Wupatki National Monument provided help, both archival and personal, along with warm hospitality, particularly Chief Ranger Kim Watson and former Wupatki rangers Larry Henderson, Wayne Landrum, and Inez Paddock (Sally Peshlakai's cousin, who translated, guided, and made terrific Navajo fry bread). Joe Wilder, son of Carleton and Judith Wilder, published an excerpt from this book in the *Journal of the Southwest*. Thank you, M., for generous assistance with funding. And thanks to Mica and Sam, for bringing us all together.

WIN THE WAR
3¢   3¢
UNITED STATES POSTAGE

Introduction: The Magic of Reality

When David and Courtney Jones moved into two upstairs rooms reached by ladder in the ruin at Wupatki National Monument, they had been married only two weeks. Except for the ruin's cement floors, which were originally hardened mud, and skylights instead of smokeholes, the rooms were exactly as they had been eight hundred years before.

David and Courtney had met in 1936, two years earlier, on a summer field trip to southwestern Indian ruins sponsored by the University of Arizona, where Davy studied archaeology and anthropology. Courtney had come out for the summer from the University of Nebraska, where she studied archaeology and ethnology.

The newlyweds became Wupatki's second full-time custodians after Jimmy and Sallie Brewer, who lived there from 1934 to 1936. Davy's first assignment for the National Park Service (NPS) was split between winter work as a ranger at Casa Grande Ruins National Monument in Coolidge, Arizona, and summer work as custodian (later called "superintendent") at Wupatki. Courtney describes that beginning in her unpublished memoirs, from which the following excerpts were taken.

> In the spring of 1938, we got married in Tucson and went to Casa Grande Ruins National Monument at Coolidge to live. It got very hot down there in the summer, so when it got almost

unbearable, we went on up to Flagstaff in this old beat-up truck we had. The next morning, Paul Beaubien came from Walnut Canyon National Monument to take us out to Wupat-ki. It was a warm morning, sunny, as we went out past the bean fields and turned off on the black cinder Sunset Crater road. We went in among the twisted trees and over the side of Sunset Crater. The boys told me all the different craters as we went along, and I remember thinking, "We'll just never get there—they're slowing down deliberately."

Pretty soon we came to the place where you can look out and see the Painted Desert, and that was going to be our view from Wupatki. It's pink and blue in the distance, and on the far horizon are what they call the Hopi Buttes. We went on winding down and down this black, sandy road for what seemed like forever. It got more and more desertlike, but it's a colorful desert, and I grew to love the colors of that country. The only trouble with the first sight of it was that it got later and later, near noon, which is a terrible time to see any desert.

If you are going to the desert, you really ought to see it just after the sun comes up or just before the sun goes down. During the middle of the day, everything flattens out and gets pale and washed-out looking. We came to Heiser Spring, which was nothing but sheep troughs, and there we began to see the red rock. The rock at Wupatki is Moencopi sandstone, which means "place where the water comes out." It's a beautiful coral red, very pretty, but it was just flat and dismal that day.

After a while we came to a Navajo on a horse, who turned out to be Hal Smith. I think it's interesting that Hal was one of the first Navajos we saw. Davy had always told me about Clyde, who was the unofficial head of the family there—the main family—and Clyde dominated everybody. But Hal and Emmett were wonderful. The Navajos on the monument were out of contact with the eastern, more acculturated part of the reservation; it was wonderful to live with people who retained their old customs and morals. They were really old-fashioned Navajos of the generation before. Hal and Emmett weren't older than Clyde, but they chose more conservative ways. I

don't think they had gone to school, and I don't remember
that they ever spoke English. They wore their hair long and
done up in back, and they wore chunks of turquoise tied in
their ears with string. Like most Navajos then, they wore
Levis rather than have somebody run up the old cotton pants.
Nez ka Yazzie wore the older-style cotton pants, but he was a
medicine man.

Anyway, Hal greeted us, and I really think he was out there
because he knew we were coming, and it was a feather in his
cap to have seen me and get to be the one that told the family about it. We talked to him a few minutes, and then we
went on. Pretty soon we came to Wupatki ruin. Wupatki is
odd to approach from the back that way because it's on a peninsula of sandstone jutting into the wash from under a black
cliff. It looks like part of the rock and is not impressive unless
you come in below it. Wupatki is very large and built like all
the ruins there of flat sandstone slabs. (Our house was eventually built the same way by the CCC [Civilian Conservation
Corps].) Behind the ruin was a two-hundred-foot cliff drifted
with black sand from lava that had run out over the red sandstone.

Well, there we were, and it was hot and pale and dull, and
I was tired. I always got carsick. Anyway, we climbed the ladder, and I said, "Davy, you have to carry me over the threshold." And he did. The door was about four feet high, and
T-shaped, which means it's wider where your arms are going
through, and you have to have your head bent over, and the
level of the floor dropped off about a foot as you stepped inside. This was a difficult project, but Davy got me carried
over the threshold, and when we got inside, I saw that the
first room had a tiny skylight. The stovepipe went out
through that skylight, so it was not very bright. Then to the
right there was a step down to the kitchen, which was very
bright because it had a big skylight.

Those were the two rooms we were to live in. At the top
of the ladder was the room used as a bedroom and office, and
the beautiful sunny little kitchen. The water was in a barrel

behind a niche in the kitchen wall. You put a bowl there or a
teakettle and turned on a faucet, and the water dribbled out
clean, you hoped. Otherwise, Davy had to go up on the roof
and wrestle the big barrel out of a hole in the ruin and clean
it. It was terrible. He pumped the water in once a week, fifty-
five gallons, and that sufficed for everything. We took our
baths there unless it was a special occasion, when we would
go down to where the spring ran out at the sheep troughs.
There was more water that way, but there were apt to be
sheep and Navajos, too.

Clyde was really the mainstay of our life at Wupatki. He
was sort of the head Navajo, although I don't think he was
much older than his brothers. We saw those people a lot, almost daily. They helped us in any way that a neighbor would,
and we helped them as we could. Clyde's older wife, Sarah—
or Sally, as we called her—was, well . . . there's hardly a word
to describe her. She is a distinguished person, and whenever
there was a Sing, or ceremony, that required a woman to be a
role model for a young person, she was the one chosen. I always thought she was a big, tall matron. The strange thing
was that I later found she was tiny. She was shorter than I was.
I still can't believe it—she was larger than life and always
will be.

Clyde was kind of a homely man. He was a very kind person, and he had a good sense of his position. I think he felt
that Wupatki was his property and that the rangers—custodians, they were called—were sent there to do the paperwork
and intervene with the government and take care of details
like that while he supervised everything else.

It really was beautiful country. There was gorgeous red
rock with black cinders, plus the beautiful gray-green bushes,
and a volcano that we could see out of one window was a
lovely plum color. We could sit on the rock at the top of our
ladder and look across the Painted Desert, which was always
changing colors whenever there were clouds. We could see as
far as Winslow, sixty miles or more away, straight across. It
was beautiful country.

In the 1930s, Wupatki National Monument was an hour-and-a-half drive from Flagstaff on unpaved roads. Modern cars, with their low clearance, could never have made the last fifteen miles in from the highway. The Joneses went to town once a week on Park Service business and to get groceries and run errands. Their only neighbors were the Navajos who lived on the monument, and an exchange of friendship and help that had begun with the Brewers continued throughout the Joneses' stay at Wupatki.

The experience of those who visited the monument was utterly different from today's tours of national parks or monuments. There was nothing there except the ruins, the landscape, and the two custodians: no visitor's center, no restrooms, no food, no telephone. There were also no pamphlets, crowds, traffic, or self-guided tours. Travelers were escorted by Courtney or Davy or, in their absence, by Clyde Peshlakai. Many arrived at midday—hot, hungry, thirsty, and stunned by the isolation, the desert, and the condition of the road. They were fortunate to be met by Courtney and Davy Jones, who towed cars out of the cinders and provided solace for those who needed it, lunch from their own meager supplies, and an introduction to the life hidden in the Wupatki ruins.

In addition to acquiring an understanding of contemporary Navajo life and art from their neighbors, the Joneses had a unique opportunity to learn about anthropology, archaeology, botany, and other fields from the many scientists who came to Wupatki to study and who enlisted their help in procuring specimens of everything from scorpions to birds. They delighted in using this knowledge to make the dry, forsaken ruins come alive.

One time I spellbound myself along with the visitors. We were in the big red sandstone rocks along the ledge below the ruin, looking up at the smooth red sandstone walls against the sky, with the tiny windows, and a few roof beams sticking out, and I got to telling how the people lived in the houses and traded for shells from the Pacific, the Gulf of California, and the Gulf of Mexico, which they made into beads, and how they raised parrots from the jungles of Mexico for their feathers, and how they farmed the cinder-covered flats, raising all they needed to eat, getting their water from the wonderful spring across the wash, and how the women sat out on the rooftops in the summer or on warm days to grind their corn. Well, all of a sudden, I could see it. I suppose I had said the same things a hundred times, but this time they had the magic of reality. Davy said that was the thing to try for—the magic of reality—so that it wasn't just a guided tour of dusty ruins, but something to make people think, to make them aware of what life was like in this country in the year 1200. He could do it fairly often. I know, because people have told me.

Wupatki's Past

The main occupation of the Wupatki area dates to between A.D. 1150 and 1250,[1] although spearpoints from 8,000 and 11,000 years ago are the oldest artifacts found there.[2] Following Sunset Crater's major eruptions in 1064–1066, use of the region by the Sinagua increased due to improved moisture retention of the soil caused by the ash and cinders deposited over eight hundred square miles, and increased precipitation caused by changes in weather patterns.[3] The climate became semi-arid again by the mid-1100s, and the Wupatki area was abandoned by about 1250. Except for Hopis who traveled through (and who may have occupied the ruin for a short time after the Sinagua left),[4] the area remained unused until around 1825, when Navajos were living at Black Point, north of Crack-in-Rock Pueblo. (Crack-in-Rock ruin is now part of the monument.) Both the Navajos and the Hopis consider parts of Wupatki sacred.[5]

The first historical reference to the archaeological remains in the Wupatki Basin was made in 1851 by Lieutenant Lorenzo Sitgreaves, who was on a military expedition
seeking a route across northern New Mexico and Arizona.
A safe trail to the newly discovered gold in California was
part of the incentive. Major John Wesley Powell inspected
and wrote about the ruins in 1885.[6] In 1896, Dr. Jesse W.
Fewkes became the first archaeologist to work in the area.
He gave some of the ruins Hopi names, but somehow the
names were switched: Wupatki, the name of the biggest
ruin, means "tall house," and Wukoki, the tallest, "big and
wide house." However, popular usage made it easier to
leave them than to change them back.[7]

Dr. Harold Sellers Colton, founder (in 1926) and director of the Museum of Northern Arizona in Flagstaff (where
Courtney lived and worked during World War II), named
the Indians who lived near Sunset Crater and Walnut Canyon before and after the eruption the Sinagua, Spanish for
"without water."[8] The Anasazi, or "ancient ones" as they
were called by the Navajos, settled to the northeast of
Sunset Crater after the eruption made the land more fertile. The Sinagua, who may have learned stone masonry
from the Anasazi, built red sandstone multistory dwellings
in Wupatki that held hundreds of people.[9] Construction
began about 1120 and ended in 1195, after which the
pueblo was gradually abandoned. No one really knows
why, but environmental factors such as diminished rainfall,
a cooler climate resulting in a shortened growing season,
and loss of the fertile volcanic ash due to wind are thought
to be contributing factors.[10]

Wupatki National Monument, forty-five miles north of
Flagstaff, Arizona, was established in 1924 to protect and
preserve the area and its artifacts. Cowboys from a nearby
ranch used to put whole Indian pots on a wall of the

Wukoki ruin and shoot at them from a galloping horse, and timbers from the roofs of the ancient dwellings were being used to fire a bootlegging still. Dr. Colton and his wife, Mary Russell F. Colton, along with Samuel A. Barrett and J. C. Clarke, were instrumental in obtaining national monument status for Wupatki.[11] The main ruins were excavated and partially stabilized by the Museum of Northern Arizona. Wupatki today encompasses 2,668 documented archaeological sites.

Courtney and David Jones's neighbors in the 1930s and '40s were part of the Peshlakai family, who first came to the Wupatki area from Black Mesa in about 1825. Peshlakai Etsidi, Clyde's father, was one of the first Navajos to learn to work silver (Peshlakai means "silversmith"). After watching a silversmith who had traveled in Mexico, he crafted some of the first silver pieces made in the western Navajo country. Etsidi, who was greatly respected by both the Navajos and the whites for his justice and wisdom, represented his people in land-use disputes in 1902 and 1904 in Washington, where he met President Theodore Roosevelt.[12]

Until the U.S. Army arrived in the early 1860s, the Navajos were nomadic. Colonel Christopher "Kit" Carson's 1863 military campaign against the Navajo Nation— ordered by General James H. Carleton (the federal commander at Santa Fe) and agreed to by the Department of War and the Bureau of Indian Affairs—was intended to confine the entire population to a single reservation: Bosque Redondo on the Pecos River at Fort Sumner, New Mexico. The Navajo people had been weakened by the New Mexican slave raids, which had increased in severity since the start of the Civil War, and close to a third of the tribe were slaves.[13] Navajo men resisting the troops were killed, women and children taken captive, crops burned, and livestock destroyed. At the point of starvation, the Navajos surrendered. Of the 8,354 people who made the Long Walk of five hundred miles from the Grand Canyon area to Bosque Redondo by December 1864, more than 2,000 died—either on the way or in captivity, from disease, malnutrition, and Comanche raids. Peshlakai Etsidi, then eleven or twelve years old, made the journey with his family in 1867 after avoiding the U.S. Army for four years. (Sallie Brewer, the "honorary custodian without pay" at Wupatki before Courtney [that is, their husbands were the official custodians, but they worked just as hard], recorded one of the most detailed narratives of the Long Walk ever published.)[14]

In 1868, after five years of exile, Navajo leaders and the U.S. government signed a treaty establishing a small reservation, about one-tenth of the land they had previously claimed. The Navajos were allowed to go home. Peshlakai Etsidi returned to the Coconino Plateau in about 1870 and married soon afterward. His descendants have lived in the Wupatki Basin ever since.[15] He became a medicine man and a *nataani*, or headman, by age fifty.[16] Before his death in 1939, the monument was enlarged from 2,234 to almost 35,000 acres, including most of the Wupatki Basin and converting to NPS property the use-areas of the four major family groups who had lived in the basin for sixty-five years before the first Park Service custodians arrived. After the Jones family left Wupatki in 1949, the Navajos became an "administrative problem."[17]

According to the Joneses, when the new superintendent took Davy's place, apparently his first order was to put the Navajo families off the monument. By the early 1960s, the only Navajos still living there were Clyde Peshlakai's family.

> . . . by the mid-1960s the presence of Navajos within the Monument boundaries had become intolerable to the NPS. Correspondence of the 1960s indicates that the good will and

respect generated by the custodians of the Monument only thirty years before were outdated concepts. Gone was the recognition that the Navajo occupation of the Wupatki Basin predated that of the NPS by over half a century. The overriding issue regarding the Navajo presence was the legal basis of NPS superiority and rightful ownership of Wupatki rather than an ethical and moral recognition of the traditional Navajo use-areas that were set aside, unbeknownst to the Navajo residents, as a National Monument.

. . . Nowadays, in a complicated arrangement with the National Park Service, one Navajo family is allowed to live on the Monument and graze a small herd of sheep as a kind of living history exhibit. The current holders of this special use permit are Clyde Peshlakai's daughters. Their household includes his granddaughter, her husband, and their three sons, great-great-grandsons of Peshlakai Etsidi. Upon the deaths of these permit holders, the National Park Service will determine the future of Navajo residence at Wupatki.[18]

Clyde Peshlakai died in 1970. His ex-wife Sally Peshlakai Lee lived across the Little Colorado River from Wupatki until 1991, when she moved to a nursing home in Flagstaff. Speaking of the old days, she said,

"I try not to think about those days. My grandson tells me, 'It is gone. Now try to think of what you can do every day.' My life is always the same from being young to being old . . . always the same. What I value and appreciated in my life is for my children and grandchildren to learn the old ways. I don't think I have hard times in my life. My knees are not working too good, I can't see too good in one eye, can't hear too good. But inside me I am still young and strong—it will continue to be that way. My children make it strong for me by caring. I don't think I will become weak in mind and body. As long as my heart is beating, I will be around."

Catherine, her sister, when asked what she would like people to know of her life, said, "I am not the kind of person who has those thoughts. I fill my mind with where we will live, how I will take care of the sheep, what we are going to eat."

After Wupatki

When he returned from overseas in 1945, Davy was appointed director of the rest and recreation camp for the army at the Grand Canyon. It made a good transition between the Army Air Corps and the old life at Wupatki. When the camp closed a few months later, the Joneses returned to Wupatki for three years; this book ends with their departure. In 1947, they adopted their daughter Jane, who spent her first two years at Wupatki. Sara was born in 1951.

Davy's first job for the NPS after leaving Wupatki was to set up San Juan National Historic Site in San Juan, Puerto Rico, where the family lived for six years. After also establishing Virgin Islands National Historic Site, the Joneses spent eighteen months at Big Bend National Park in Texas. Davy then worked for the NPS branch office in Santa Fe, New Mexico, as regional planner for the Southwest area from 1956 until the late 1960s, when he began a very active retirement: He directed a thirty-four-agency study recommending ways for state and local governments of northern New Mexico to protect the Embudo watershed; he led a fundraising drive to restore the centuries-old church in Las Trampas, a traditional Hispanic town; and he worked for the antiwar movement during the Vietnam era.

Courtney's life has been equally busy. She was active in the antiwar movement and worked for the Santa Fe Museum of Fine Arts in the Spanish colonial department and as an associate editor of *Landscape Magazine*. She continues her involvement in the Santa Fe community, in politics, and in writing.

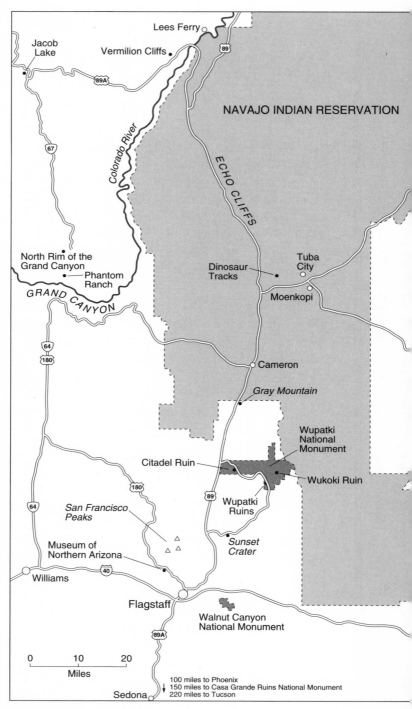

Northeastern Arizona

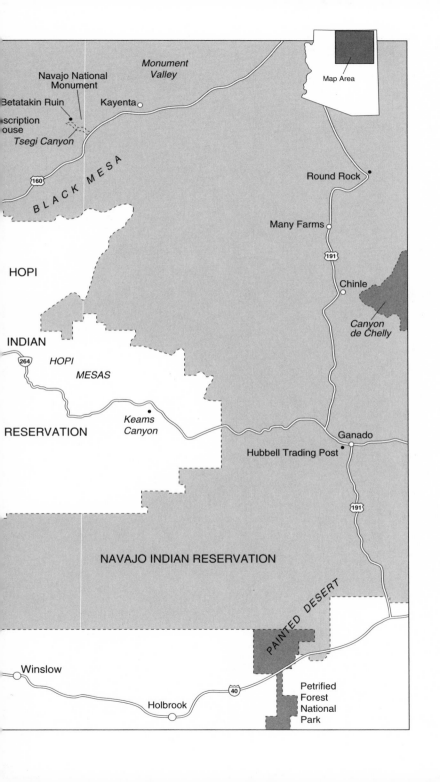

Letters from Wupatki

Dear Gagoo and Aunt Clara,

. . . We are still working on the flower collection—I
never thought I'd have to be a botanist! It is very interesting work. We go out and dig up the blooming plant, root
and all (unless it is a tree), then trim off unnecessary leaves
and blooms and arrange it so that at least one flower and
bud show up well, also a leaf right-side up and one wrong-
side up. Then we make notes as to the locality, type of soil,
altitude, and whether they are abundant or sparse. When
we get back we have to go through them, catalogue them
and make a card for each. We have over sixty kinds at present. Duplicates will be sent to be identified and then they
will be mounted in Berkeley and we will keep them on file
here. There are many beautiful flowers, some very showy.
There is an orange mallow now in bloom which makes the
whole countryside orange. Most of the hills here are covered with black volcanic cinder, with outcroppings of
bright red sandstone. The wildflowers show up well on
this, as do the junipers, pines, and small green bushes. It is
very handsome country, though quite different from anything I had ever seen.

I am trying to entice the birds with crumbs and water,
and every morning and evening I carry water to some of
the big sandstone rocks with cavities in them. There are
some nice natural birdbaths around the ruin—the only dif-
ficulty being that the stone absorbs the water and it also
evaporates quickly. There is a Say's Phoebe nest in a rock
beside our privy. Two of the eggs hatched today and it is
going to be interesting to watch the little birds. We shall
band them before they learn to fly. They say that with the
proper traps we will be able to band more migrating birds

(*above*) Wupatki from the north, 1937. The arrows point to the newly excavated apartment and the porch. (*below*) Wupatki from the east, circa 1937. Davy sent these photos to Courtney before their wedding. (Photographs by Milton "Jack" Snow)

than anyone in the country as they all stop at the spring here. So next summer if the robins in the yard wear brace-lets, you will know who is responsible.

. . . This is such a nice little house in the ruin. We will take pictures of the inside soon so you all can see the "oldest inhabited house in the United States." We have only a two-burner stove at present, which certainly taxes my ingenuity. However, Davy seems to like my cooking. I can't bake bread in this present situation as the heat in the oven varies all the time, but it turns out some good biscuits, cornbread, and cookies. . . .

Wupatki
July 1938

Dear Gagoo and Aunt Clara,

. . . Columbus [Nebraska] must be lovely and green after the rains, and I hope your nice weather continues. Big fluffy clouds come up every day and often we can see five or six rainstorms, but so far it is just hot and dusty here.

About a week ago we went to town a new way—around the back of the San Francisco Peaks. It was quite a good Forest Service road and the scenery was magnificent. We went through several aspen forests where the white-trunked trees were so thick we couldn't see out and the ground was covered with big ferns. . . .

The Nichols[1] left yesterday. Meals seem rather quiet now. Just before they left we had quite a literary spree. Mary Jane wrote up the bird observations for the month, Davy wrote an article on the yucca and its moth, and I wrote about the Rock Wren family. These were all sent to Headquarters [at Coolidge] and will be published in the *Monthly Report.*[2] The yucca article is fine and I think Davy writes exceptionally well. It is about how the moth lays its eggs in the yucca blossom and packs them in with pollen. As the seeds which are thus fertilized ripen, the moth-worms live on some of them. The plant depends on the insect for its pollination, the moth depends on the yucca for food & lodging—it's the most remarkable interdependency between plants and insects.

My warp yarn is finished and soon I shall set up my loom.[3] I am going to gather some rabbit brush today sometime so I can dye some of the wool—it should be a yellow-green at this time of year. It takes about five hours to prepare the dye but it should be most interesting work.

Wupatki
September 25, 1938

Dear Gagoo and Aunt Clara,

. . . Last week we went to town a day late (Wednesday) as on Tuesday some engineers came out to plan a new road. They do that every month or so but their ideas change so fast that we are not counting on a new road for a couple of years. . . . While we were in town on Wednesday we were informed that we were to take the new ranger up to Navajo National Monument the next day. We were thrilled, as that is one of the great beauty spots of Arizona and so far from civilization that few people ever see it. It is in the Tsegi [Navajo for "rocky canyon"] Canyons near Monument Valley, just this side of the Utah line. . . .

In the morning we got the ranger and his mother, who wanted to go along, and were all ready to leave when Dr. Colton[4] of the Museum [of Northern Arizona] said he wanted to come out that afternoon and excavate some skeletons which the CCC [Civilian Conservation Corps] boys had uncovered while digging us a new privy. Since

Courtney and Davy at their wedding, Tucson, Arizona, April 20, 1938 (Photograph by Tad Nichols)

the truck was packed, we took Mr. Wetherill[5] and his
mother out to Wupatki to stay until we could go to
Navajo.

That afternoon Dr. Colton and some friends arrived, excavated the skeletons, and invited us all to go on a steak
fry. So we all went off into the pinyon trees and had a big
bonfire and steaks and beans.

Friday morning we were on the road at 8:00 a.m.—Mrs.
Wetherill and I rode in the back of the truck on the sleeping bags and groceries—the ranger can get supplies only
once a month, so we had a big load. It was a beautiful day
and the scenery is some of the grandest in the state. We
crossed the Painted Desert just above where it becomes the
Grand Canyon, passed the Hopi country, and went up on
the high plateaus. The main feature of Navajo is Betatakin
["ledge house"] Ruin. This, one of the most beautiful and
perfect ruins in the country, is built in a huge, perfectly
arched cave in the wall of the canyon. The plateau above is
a desert; the canyon is a regular jungle of vines, ferns, pines
and aspen trees. A spring just below the ruin supplies
plenty of ice-cold water for the ranger and the visitors. We
had to pack the bedrolls and some of the food down a trail
built along the face of the cliff about a mile and a quarter.
Before supper we walked around the ruins and explored the
canyon. In the morning we rose about 4:30 and after
breakfast we visited other ruins and saw many ancient
paintings on the rocks. Then we packed our things back up
the trail and had Mrs. Wetherill home in Flagstaff before
2:00 p.m. It was a wonderful trip and though our muscles
are still sore, we are very glad we could go.

Yesterday some visitors were here all day. I went down
to the river with them, where they traded several cases of
home-canned fruit to the Navajos for a rug. . . .

Coolidge
February 26, 1939

Dear Gagoo,

. . . Our living room has three big windows on one side and we have lots of fun watching the Gambel sparrows feed on the grain we put out. And I have suet tied on the branches of the bushes and the big cactus wrens come and stab at it with their long curved bills—they are the largest wrens—a little bigger than a robin. I have been trying to band some birds but I always feel "the wren and the phoebe *are* smarter than we be," for I lose better ones than I catch. It was the saddest day when I actually held an Arizona Pyrrhuloxia (big red and gray cardinal) in my hand and he got loose. I am keeping all the bird banding files for the monument—it is most interesting but takes about an hour a day. . . .

Davy and I were in Phoenix the first of the week. . . . It

Wupatki from the northwest, 1939 (Photograph by Natt Dodge, courtesy of Wupatki National Monument)

was fun to be in a city, but we are both glad we don't live in one. We may get a lovely trip in March—about eight days driving to the Grand Canyon, Petrified Forest, some of the southern monuments and to El Paso, with the Superintendent and a lady from the Washington office. . . .

Wupatki
April 1939

Dear Gagoo and Aunt Clara,

We enjoyed hearing from you and thank you so much for the lovely anniversary card—it hardly seems possible that it has been a whole year for the time has flown so quickly.

It is just grand to have Edna [Courtney's sister, also called "Liz"] with us. . . . The other day we went to inspect an eagle's nest and she hung head-down over the cliff while we held her feet so she could see the baby eagle. The way she can climb around and do all these things is wonderful and of course makes her trip all the more interesting, as she will not miss a thing. I am a terrible climber, and always said it was probably due to being raised on the plains, but now I have no alibi. . . .

Last weekend we went to one of the most beautiful and isolated spots in Arizona—Monument Valley and Navajo National Monument. There were four of us, Sallie Brewer,[6] wife of the ranger at Navajo; Katharine Bartlett,[7] technician at the Museum of Northern Arizona; Edna and I. . . . We went to Cameron and Tuba City, taking a little side trip to a Hopi village [Moenkopi] and some dinosaur tracks. Then we went to Kayenta—the farthest town from a railroad in the U.S.—and over a hundred miles from a paved road. . . . We went out about fifteen miles into Monument Valley and it was a striking sight as there were lots of beautiful cloud effects. We got to Navajo in time to

Betatakin Ruin, Navajo National Monument (Photograph by John L. Blackford)

fix supper, and put our bedrolls out under some pinyons and junipers. The moonlight was beautiful and [we] were surprised at being rained on a bit during the night. The next day we walked around the rim of Betatakin Canyon and looked down on the ruin. . . . The views along the trail are magnificent. The Tsegi river has cut canyons over a thousand feet deep, with perpendicular walls of red sand-

stone. . . . We ate lunch in the ruin and climbed all around
it and went into many of the little rooms, which are so perfectly preserved that it seems they have been deserted only
a few weeks ago. We got out of the canyon in time to
move our beds into a deserted Navajo hogan, and fix supper before dark. Yesterday we learned to pitch horseshoes
and finally got started home before noon. I am so glad
Edna could have this trip as it is certainly one of the most
marvellous experiences in the state and few people have
the opportunity to see and appreciate it. . . .

Wupatki
late July 1939

Dear Gagoo and Father,
    . . . We are busier this summer than last, but it is really
fascinating work and there is so much to learn about the
country that we enjoy every minute. . . . The people who
come out here all do such interesting things and we enjoy
talking with them. . . .
    My rug is about four inches high now—I just wish I
could go down to the hogan every day, but so far have
managed only three trips. [The Peshlakais] are living about
a mile away, and Sally[8] and I have looms under a juniper
tree. We have blankets stretched over the branches above
to augment the shade, and there is a lovely view of the
desert down the little canyon. They are very patient with
me and I am beginning to understand what is going on—
they weave so fast that one has no idea how many little
processes they must go through to weave one thread. I am
glad to get a chance to learn one of the crafts of the na-
tives and it is most interesting to be there with the Navajos. Guess I will never learn the language, though, as the
sounds are so different from those used in English. . . .
    I guess I told you how we had to catch scorpions for a

Sally Peshlakai weaving at an outside shelter, August 1938
(Photograph by Tad Nichols)

man who was studying them, and keep them alive to send
to him. Well, it was quite a job, keeping the horrid little
things around and finding food for them but we are
rewarded—the man found that we had three new species
and wrote that he had named one *Wupatkiensis* for the ruin
and one *Jonesii* for Davy! Isn't that rare. I am still catching
the awful animals, but we just preserve them now. . . .

[From the *Superintendent's Monthly Report* of July 24, 1939:
"Like the Navajo children, the Wupatki scorpions have
been away to school and returned with white man's names.
From the material we have sent, Mr. H. L. Stahnke of Iowa
State College has discovered three new species: *Vejovis
wupatkiensis, Vejovis jonesii,* and *Hadrurus spadicis.*"]

Wupatki
November 1939

Dear M.,

. . . I wish you could see the mansion—no, it won't be finished till spring at the earliest—but the roof is on and wonderful exotic pieces of plumbing are scattered all over the ground, and it is very exciting to say the least. [The new house was not completed until three years later.] The house is simply beautiful—according to the report it may not be entirely comfortable—but I really have never seen anything quite so swell—it's the decorator's dream. It looks like it should be filled with the most modern and simple things, like lucite furniture, but of course a little ingenuity should take the place of those. I'd love to get some ideas from you—since seeing the swell results you produce from practically a shoestring—so if you do get back here in the near future we'd like to hire you to help decorate—not a lucrative job, but we can offer board, room and scenery. Since I had fair success spinning and weaving a rug this summer, I'm all inspired to make some upholstery in diagonal twill or whatever it's called. New patios spring up around the house almost every day—there's a partly paved, partly native-planted courtyard in front, a patio between the house and museum, and the main patio which the house is built around, and which may have a pond and trees. The other day we had a visit from the architect—if I had known he was coming, I fear I should have been trembling in a distant canyon after writing that danged report—but he was just a nice guy, and we had lots of fun with him.

We took this man, neatly dressed in a dark blue suit, on a wild trip to Crack-in-the-Rock ruin—the glory of the Southwest—which is reached by means of an old Navajo road hacked out by hand for wagon traffic, and is really a lulu. But that ruin is worth it or anything—it's up on an

overhanging mesa, and is reached by a little trail through a
crack, which is guarded by a wall with loopholes. Then in
one of the rooms is a little hole in the floor, which leads to
an underground passage just big enough to wiggle through,
and which leads out down below in another room. Just like
you always hope a ruin will be. . . .

The *New Yorker* is marvellous—and did I tell you what a
tremendous circulation our copy has? It goes to Sallie
Brewer, a hundred miles from paving, then to the trader at
Shonto, then, I think, to the people at Rainbow Bridge
[National Monument, in Utah], and has at least one other
reader.

The Navajos are all fine—the Peshlakai family has been
increased to the extent of a son and heir, named, in
English, Charley Clyde [Catherine's baby]. The little boys
get cuter all the time, and come in to visit and look at the
catalogues every now and then. . . . one day Emmett
[Kellam], Clyde's half-brother and nephew from across the
river, paid us a visit with an interpreter and Clyde came in
too. After about an hour of looking at catalogues, Emmett
shyly pulled out a sack, from which he took a little rug.
On it is a picture—the foreground is liberally covered with
saguaro cacti, and a road winds over the horizon and in the
sky are many geometrical clouds, and from the black border a black line extends a few inches down from the top.
"What is this?" we said, and Emmett said, "A picture." Then
he said the cactus were a kind that grew down near Phoenix and Tucson, and that the road was a *"chiddy ba teen,"*
which means car trail. Finally we asked what the black line
in the sky was, and Clyde broke in with "Jesus Savior, I
guess!" When the shouts of laughter ceased echoing, we
decided . . . [to] send [the rug] on to Great Neck to remind you of God's country.

Our weather is still grand, in spite of a bit of snow on
the Peaks, and the visitors still drive in occasionally. The

Courtney in the ruin pantry, 1940 (Photograph by Natt Dodge)

CCC camp is installed at Heiser Spring, and Wupatki seems a hive of activity with trucks rumbling along and the boys yelling at their work—and at night the camp is lighted up like a regular city—imagine the incongruity of electric lights out here. They even have irons, and I went over and pressed a skirt one day. But we are still isolated from war news, thank goodness—someone did try to sell us a radio, and brought one out on approval—but it did sound too funny to hear jazz emanating from a ruin. . . .

[From the *Monthly Report* of May 25, 1939: "While we are anxious to see the house completed, we shall not move out of the quarters in the ruin without misgivings. At present there is a bond between us and the 'old people' in that it is our home too. A year from now I am afraid that Wupatki will impress me as more of a ruin. In addition, living in the ruin, we have a better opportunity of 'contacting' our visitors. You would be surprised what friendships will spring up after an hour in our quarters."]

Wupatki
February 11, 1940

Dear Aunt Liz,

. . . Had quite a busy time the last couple of weeks. We went on a picnic to inspect the ruins, taking cocoa in the new thermos, and wienies to roast on the forks. We ate in Grandfather's rock hogan at the old farm in the canyon. The house had a little wall fireplace and it worked fine. Then we found a new ruin! It is down by the river and I guess it is off the monument. There was a hole where someone had dug, probably years ago, and some of the dirt had fallen in and uncovered a lovely wooden ladle. We took pictures of it in place, but we couldn't bring it back as we had nothing to carry it in. So we covered it with dirt, as it looked like rain. Sent in a note for Dr. Colton to come out the next day if he wanted to, and we would take it out. He couldn't come, so we went down in a pouring rain, with a brisk wind, and took out the ladle and wrapped it in cotton.

Went up to Sunset Crater the next day, and had to put on chains to get through the snow. . . . That night a man who has a cattle ranch near here came in and we had him to dinner and he told us stories about the old times around here. The next day the Range Rider from Cameron came up to see about water for the Navajos. His wife and little girl were with him and we had them to lunch, and had a nice visit with them. Each district on the reservation has a Range Rider, to keep track of the Navajos and how many sheep they have and so on.

On Sunday Milton Wetherill and his mother came out—as usual, and we had them to lunch. The old lady about gets me down with her constant chatter, and they stayed all day. Davy took Milton down to see the new ruin, and he scraped around in the hole and found a big bowl with a squash in it, and arrow points, and a couple of little baskets. He works for the Museum and wants Dr. Colton to excavate the ruin right away. That hole must have been dug into a burial, and the digger just didn't go very far. . . .

The head of the publicity dept. in Washington, Miss Story, who was with us on that trip last spring, recommended me to the *Christian Science Monitor*, along with four other women who have exciting lives, and they asked me to write an article about living in the ruin.[9] They will pay 15 dollars so I am sure going to try. But I don't have much confidence in my writing, since all last month I tried to write a story about rug weaving for the *Report*, and had to throw it away. If this place will settle down to something less like a three-ring circus, maybe I can do it. Do you have any ideas? I get so used to living here that I forget what would be interesting to anyone else. . . .

Wupatki
early March 1940

Dear Lizzy Begay,

. . . Paul [Beaubien][10] loaned us some old books on Arizona, by some of the early explorers, and they are just rare. The description of the country along the Little Colorado and what is now the monument is the wildest thing I ever

Courtney in the ruin kitchen, 1940 (Photograph by Natt Dodge)

read and if you think I exaggerate, you should see this. It is the country at its worst, in the midst of a dust storm, and the writer thinks the Indians must have been crazy to live here.

We are going to take some pictures of the inside of our house (ruin) this noon if there aren't too many visitors. I want Davy to take one of me sweeping because now I wear a dust mask, or silica filter. It looks like a gas mask and is very uncomfortable but it keeps me from sneezing and coughing. Every time I write home I think we will have some pictures to send, but the boy who is printing them just doesn't seem to get anything done. We have about eight rolls of film in town, and Davy says the negatives are perfect, but I can never make out what they would look like. . . .

Davy has applied for his Yale fellowship, and we should know whether we are going by April. I can hardly wait, and surely hope he gets it, as if we move into the house we might not get a chance to go for years. The house has all but the living room floors in and looks like a house really. It is just darling, much prettier than we expected. The fireplace doesn't work, but they still have time to rebuild it, T.G. But alas—there are 144 panes of glass in the living room alone. And the glass door isn't in yet. We will have to hire a janitor. . . .

We climbed Doney the other day, and it is simply marvellous. Better than the top of Sunset Crater for view. Up on top are some ruins—what on earth did they do for water—and a big "squeeze-up" [a place where lava squeezes up through cracks in the hardening lava crust] coming right up out of the cinders. All the rocks are bombs, which fell back on top of the crater, and they are long and twisted into funny shapes. From the top you can see the entire monument, and for once I almost got my directions straight. . . .

They tell us that the only way we can save the country around here from drying up and blowing away is to have the Navajos take their sheep over across the river on the reservation for six months during the growing season—we hate to have them have to do that, but the sheep will not get anything to eat if they keep on grazing here all the time. They think in two years the country will be all right if they do this, so it is for their own good. The Forest Service men caught Clyde with the sheep on the forest land one day and told him to keep them off. Davy was talking to Clyde about it, and finally Clyde said, "What do they want to do there, plant watermelons and corn?" . . .

[From the *Superintendent's Monthly Report*, May 24, 1940: "The Navajos have moved off the Monument for the summer months to improve the range and are now living in the sandy wastes along the Little Colorado River. Considerable credit is due the Peshlakai and Hal Smith families for their cooperation in this respect. Last winter it was brought to their attention that some of the lands are being overgrazed. Instead of taking a belligerent attitude as they have with the Navajo Service, they wanted to cooperate. When it appeared that the only solution was to move off during the growing season for the next two years, they agreed."

And October 27, 1940: "The Navajos are delighted with the abundance of feed on the Monument and apparently their sheep are too. For almost a week after they moved back on the Monument the sheep grazed within half a mile of the hogans—unprecedented in this country."]

Wupatki
March 14, 1940

Dear Aunt Clara and Gagoo,
. . . We had a blizzard last Sunday—it snowed so hard we couldn't see a thing, but melted as it fell. . . . Spring must really be here now—our summer birds are coming back, new ones every day, and it is good to hear them sing. We are watching our rock wrens closely to see whether they raise two broods a year. They gather tiny stones and make a floor for their nests by paving a little cave in a boulder. Then they build a little stone wall in front so the babies can't fall out. The robins and bluebirds are leaving us for the North.

The Sierra Club, a hiking group from California, is coming to look over Wupatki sometime within a week. Davy is going to take them all over the monument. We got in practice yesterday by climbing a big crater near here. Had never climbed it before and it was thrilling. From the top we could see the entire monument, as well as landmarks of the Navajo and Hopi reservations. The coloring was lovely—the crater itself is actually purple and all our canyons are rose color, and of course the Painted Desert was quite a display. When it warms up, I will have to try watercolor sketches again. . . .

Wupatki

March 1940

Dear Folksies,

. . . Now for the sad news—Davy got a letter from Yale yesterday, saying that he had good qualifications, but that due to strong competition he would not get a fellowship this year. So we will not be going East, but Davy really doesn't seem to mind at all. He is getting more and more interested in handling the monument work, and I believe he is rather relieved that he is going to be here next winter. Of course it is a relief financially, as the house is ready to be plastered, and they will probably have it finished in a couple of months, even allowing for re-doing it a couple of times. Now we are able to get thrilled about furnishing it, and sit around planning furniture most of the time. I only wish my mamma and papa could get out to see us while we are still in the ruin, but maybe it would be more fun for you when we are in the house—and of course it would be more comfortable. . . .

When we went to town last Tuesday we took Sally Peshlakai, and I had quite a time with her. We usually leave

Courtney and Davy in the living room of the ruin, 1940
(Photograph by Tad Nichols)

her at the grocery store, and pick her up when we go
home, but this time I met her wandering around town in
the afternoon. . . . Lois [Beaubien] and I took her with us
to get Cokes . . . it was fun to see what a kick she got out
of looking at all the different stores. We took her to eat
with us and Paul and Lois at a cafe, and she said she didn't
have any money so we would tease her and tell her we
would take her silver buttons off to pay the bill.[11]

When we got to the monument entrance our lights went
out. Davy had an extra fuse, which he put in, and it blew out
when we were two miles in. So we drove the last ten miles in

(left to right) Frank Pinkley ("The Boss"); Ruth (Rudi) Egermeyer,
wife of the chief ranger at Casa Grande Ruins National
Monument; and Natt Dodge, National Park Service regional
naturalist, at Coolidge (Photographer unknown, courtesy of
Courtney Reeder Jones)

total darkness, except for a weak little flashlight which Davy
held out the window. It certainly was thrilling bouncing
along at about two miles an hour, and Davy was glad he
knew the road. Sally was simply petrified, and kept sort of
moaning and shrieking every time we went around a curve. I
don't know when I have been so glad to see our little ruin.

Wupatki
April 15, 1940

Dear Lizzy Begay,
    . . . Did you know that Hugh Miller[12] is the new superin-
tendent? We are all so glad because things will go on just as
they always have, and Hugh will try to carry out all the Boss's

ideas.[13] The Boss had asked that Hugh be the next supt. so
we are real glad that they didn't get someone else. The assistant hasn't been chosen, but that doesn't matter so much. . . .

We are hoping to get down there [to Tucson] the end of
this month, as there is to be a science conference—archaeology and anthropology, which would be fine for Davy to
attend. Maybe we will get permission to go on business, so
I could go too, but otherwise just Davy will go, by taking
leave and going with someone or on the train. . . .

I got a letter from the *Christian Science Monitor*, accepting
my article, although they may cut it. They didn't pay me
yet, as they want permission to use Tad's [Nichols] pictures
or we will send them some. I will get at least fifteen dollars
for it, which will be swell for the house furnishing. The
Pow-Wow Program accepted and will use my article on
weaving,[14] and I am trying to sell it to the *Arizona Highways*,
along with some of Davy's pictures. Oh, it was wonderful
to see some of Davy's pictures all enlarged for the Program!
And everyone was just crazy about them—they all say
they are the best Navajo pictures they have seen, and the
photographer says they are the best negatives he has ever
enlarged. I surely hope Davy will get to have a darkroom
here because if he does his own work it will be just what
he wants, and not half so expensive. . . .

On the way home we stopped to visit Clyde and Sally.
They are in their new house—Clyde built a two-room
rock house, with windows, which is really very nice, made
like ours. They have their "sitting room stove" now, which
Jimmy Kay[15] gave Sally for the lovely rug she wove him.
Charley Clyde is just a darling baby, and so smart. He is a
little scared of me, but just loves Davy, and shakes hands
with him all the time. Sally let me weave on a rug she was
making, and I remembered how all right. I am going to try
to make our upholstery for the new house. . . .

It is hard to believe that it is about a year ago that you

Courtney, Charley Clyde, and Sally Peshlakai with a rug Sally
made for Jimmy Kay, 1938 (Photograph by Tad Nichols)

came up to visit. You wouldn't know it was the same season. It gets up around 80 in the shade now, and there is
hardly ever any wind, and all the flowers are blooming. I
hope we aren't going to have so much wind like last
year. . . .

Wupatki
mid-April 1940

Dear Folksies, and everybody,
    . . . We are going to Tucson! Imagine! Davy got leave to
go to the scientific conference [American Anthropological
and Archaeological Society]. . . . I am going to look at all

the furniture and stuff in the stores, as it will probably be the last chance in a city before we move in. . . .

We are so glad not to be hearing war news—it is bad enough in the magazines. When you are around the radio, you feel like you have to listen all the time, and we heard it a lot in town. We went in Monday night so Davy could mail some things, and then stayed at Paul's. And believe it or not—there was a blizzard! We were quite unprepared, but it

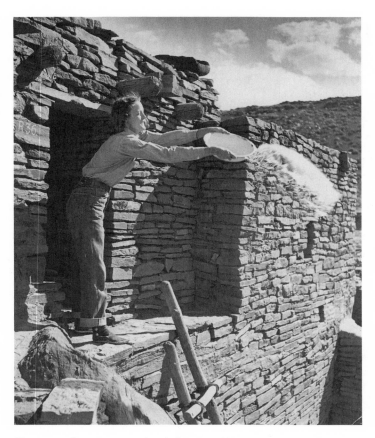

Courtney throwing out the dishwater (Photograph by Tad Nichols)

melted in town almost as fast as it fell. . . . We didn't even have rain when they had all the snow in town, but we had wind—at times on Monday it blew an average of 50 mph. Throwing out the [dish]water was really something. . . .

For our anniversary Davy is making me with his own hands some beautiful hickory weaving tools! He couldn't resist telling me, but I haven't seen them yet. . . . It is hard to believe we have been married two years come next Saturday. The time has gone so quickly and we have had so much fun. We are going to have a nice dinner here—I got a pork roast, and am going to surprise Davy with his favorite avocados, the first of the season. . . . I made a drawing for a bookplate for Davy, and am having a cut made to have it printed, and got him a book he wanted to really surprise him. He got me some wonderful colored pencils which you can paint with too—he gave them to me already, as I was doing some sketches for him the other day. They are just grand and make me want to draw all the time.

We are sending some pictures. . . . Davy took the aspens last fall up on the Peaks with the photographer from Prescott. I took the one of Davy under the pines on top of Sunset just after we got back from Nebraska. That is what the top of the crater looks like, and we brought down the sign he is sitting on for the winter. The other is of Wukoki Ruin, and Davy's bookplate will have a drawing of it from the same angle. It is the prettiest ruin on the monument, a four-story watch tower [that] looks off toward the river. . . .

Wupatki
May 1940

Dear Folks,

. . . Wednesday afternoon some Indian Service men came out to talk to Davy about fixing up a place by the river for the Navajos to farm by irrigation. They want to dam the river a little bit, enough to divert the water into canals, when there is any water. It is just grand to have that come up at this time when we were trying to get the Navajos to move down to the river. They will all have jobs while they build the dam, and will feel so important getting to participate in this experiment. I can just imagine how Clyde will instruct the Indian Service as to where and how the dam should be built. . . .

They have to finish the house by June 30, so we will be in real soon. When they get all the cement mixers and junk moved, I will try to take some pictures of it. . . . I am anxious for them to finish the cupboards and closets—it doesn't look like there would be room to put away a handkerchief, but I think all new houses look that way when they are empty, and when I think of how our things are stuffed into one dresser and one wardrobe now, I realized that we will probably have more space than we can fill. . . .

Wupatki
May 1940

Dear Lizzy Begay,

. . . The meetings [in Tucson] were just fine. I have been trying to get good weaving wool for Sally so she can make some more real nice rugs, so I went to the agriculture meetings because a man was talking about the wool experiments. I got to meet him and am going to get some wool from Window Rock, at least enough so Sally can make us a big rug for our living room. The last afternoon we went to town and looked at furniture. You know we wanted to make the davenport and a chair by making a frame and putting rope springs on it, and a mattress. They have just exactly that, but the things are for a patio, and have wheels, so we just looked at them real carefully and got a catalogue so we know just how to make them. . . .

We saw so many people we knew from all over the Southwest . . . Jean [McWhirt], Addison [Pinkley], M.—who has practically sold the ranch, and may be up soon to look for another around here!—and Ruth [Rudi] and Don [Egermeyer][16] . . . . They just love Saguaro [National Monument], and Ruth is banding birds and Don is making study skins. . . . Judie and Carleton Wilder[17] will be up soon to be at the Grand Canyon. . . .

The mockingbirds got back yesterday and are just singing their heads off. They still sit, a pair of them, on the black rock across the canyon from the john, and sing and then fly up into the air singing. The rock wrens have nested in the old place in Room 7, and have four babies. They all seem earlier than last year, but maybe the time just goes so fast that we don't realize how late it is. The Apache plume is already almost through blooming and has plumes. We have had some of those terrible strong winds, but not like last year, and lately there have been real quiet summery days. . . .

Imagine this—we are going to the Grand Canyon! . . . Davy is being sent to the Fire School to learn how to prevent and extinguish forest fires. . . . [We'll] go up to the Canyon by the old stagecoach road. I think it is the one that goes around the Peaks; at least you get on it somewhere over there near the mountains, and it will probably be in awful condition but we have always wanted to take it and it goes by some old ranches and through some different country. It should be a pretty drive now that the wildflowers are coming out. . . .

Wupatki
June 1940

Dear Folksies and Liz the W.,

. . . It was a very nice birthday, grand weather and we had cake and fried chicken, and Davy gave me a pair of

Picnic on a trip to Moenkopi, near Tuba City, summer 1938: *(left
to right)* Tad Nichols, Davy, Courtney, Judie Wilder, and Carleton
Wilder (Photograph by Mary Jane Nichols)

wool cards so my weaving tools are almost complete. . . .
The darndest dust storm just came up from the river.
Haven't been able to see the desert all day, but it was
mostly smoke from some big forest fires south of Flag, and
now the dust. Until today it has been 103 degrees every afternoon in the Wupatki Weather Station, and there are big
clouds, but they just lightning and thunder. That is why
the forest fires—they had 70 men down in Long Valley
yesterday, and were calling for more. None of the fires was
very big, but there were lots of them. That is where the elk
are. . . .

The Coles,[18] who were here last summer, are back at the
College, where he is teaching leather and metal work.

Golly, how we wish we could take his courses. . . . He says if we get time, he will show us how to make things out of copper—which is a help, as we wanted to have copper tops on our end tables. . . .

We are looking for Judie and Carleton to come in any time now—they are all settled at the Canyon for another summer. Carleton got his degree this spring. It is nice to have so many of our friends around now.

During the Pow-Wow they are sending up someone from Coolidge to help Davy with the guiding. He will take Sunset Crater, and whoever comes up will do Wupatki. It will be fairly ghastly, since Davy will have to go over bright and early every morning and take a lunch, and come back late. But he is anxious to find out just what the Sunset visitors are like, as that will be the next place to get fixed up. Today he is finishing an exhibit for the Citadel [ruin], and he and the new CCC boy will go over and install it this afternoon.

Wupatki
June 18, 1940

Dear Gagoo and Aunt Clara,

. . . Our Navajos have been away a long time, and it seems strange now not to have them around. Saturday afternoon Davy had to go to Cameron on business, and on the way we stopped at a trading post. There were Sally, Clyde, Catherine [Clyde's second wife and Sally's sister], and the baby, and we surely had a reunion. Sally came running out and hugged me, much to the amusement of the tourists. They don't plan to be back here till fall, but we hear that their corn is coming up down at the river, so they will be around for the harvest. Clyde was out in back of the trading post nailing some boards together. He said he was making a "rabbit hogan"—they have bought four black-and-white tame rabbits for the baby.

They are starting to paint the inside of the house today. When they quit work at four I will hurry over to see how it looks. Last week they stained the beams and they are the prettiest I have ever seen. They are yellow pine, with the knots and defects left on, and they just rubbed them with a grayish stain, which makes them look weathered. The walls will be white and ivory mixed half and half, and the floor, alas, is dark red linoleum. I say alas, because it is one of those shades which will show every footprint, and I don't want to feel like following my guests around with a dust-mop. But it is a small matter when the rest of the house is so nice. It will probably be completed the end of this month, but we do not expect to move in until August or September. It is rumored that we will have venetian blinds! We have been washing our hair and clothes in the drive-way back of the garage where the water is installed—much more convenient than walking a mile and hauling the water.

We are fixing up an exhibit for the Citadel Ruin, so that the people who come in just the first five miles will have some idea of what it is all about. Davy is fixing labels and pictures for it and I made a little map. My only other project at the time is trying to knit a sweater for the Red Cross, and I am really trying to get it finished soon. . . .

Wupatki
[late July 1940]

Dear Folksies and Liz,

. . . On Saturday the Coles [Butler and Lee] came out, and fortunately we had very few visitors, so we had a real good time with them. Davy and But went over to the new house and fixed up a table to work on and Davy got a leather box all cut out. They will come out again before they leave and Davy can learn to carve a design on it. But made one with a Navajo silver design on it, and is going to set three turquoises in the top—very lovely and unusual. Clyde Peshlakai came over and watched him carve a belt, and was very interested. But would like to get a job in the Indian Service teaching the Navajos more crafts—some of the boys here are clever at making miniature saddles, and would like to learn to do more with leather. It is going to be a grand hobby for Davy during the long winter evenings. He really needs something like that to take his mind off the *Reports*.

Sally Peshlakai came over on Monday with a good interpreter and I surely enjoyed getting to really visit with her. Then she went over to her house to do some sewing— wanted me to go along, but I didn't have anything cut out, although it was too bad to miss the chance.

When she left she noticed a tiny deer mouse in the room below. We left it there and that afternoon there were three more. We fed them some milk and left them there to see if their parents got them during the night, but evidently the mother had been killed as there weren't any tracks in the morning. So we fixed them up in a box, and fed them milk with a medicine dropper. One had died during the night. While we were in town Leslie, the CCC boy, fed them. That night another one died, but we had two of the precious little things. They were really just darling, although I can imagine Mother won't think so. They got so they could climb up in our hands and hold the medicine dropper, and then sit up and wash their faces. They were real cute and frisky until yesterday, when they seemed to go into a decline. Guess the milk just didn't agree with them or something, and this morning they were both dead.

Davy putting a roof on the refrigerator room (next to the apartment in the ruin), 1938 (Photograph by Tad Nichols)

I sure miss them, because I was feeding them every two hours, but suppose they wouldn't have been able to survive when we turned them loose. . . .

Sally Peshlakai went to town with us. . . . We came out without stopping for supper, and it was getting dark when we got here. When we started up to the hogan, there was a big pool of water in a low place in the canyon. It has a clay bottom, and Davy had been stuck in it before, so we just had to stop. Sally left all her groceries in the truck, and she and Haskie Yazzie had to walk about half a mile. We turned around and started home, and darn it, we had a flat tire. It was good and dark then, but Davy got it changed and we finally got home, put away the groceries and had a supper. The next day Sally sent three men over on horse-back to get her things. Now they are moving farther away again. Clyde didn't think it would rain again this summer, but yesterday it rained over half an inch. . . .

We have run out of bread this week, which just delights Davy as I am making rolls. . . . The only trouble is that using the oven makes this tiny kitchen so hot—but in an-other month we won't be eating in this kitchen. . . .

Wupatki
late July 1940

Dear Folksies and Liz the W.,

. . . When we came back from town Tuesday, we real-ized it had rained here, as the road was badly washed [out]; in fact, the one up the hill to the ruin was just three or four little canyons. And it had rained 3/4 of an inch! It has just been perfect ever since, cool and clear and lovely, with big soft clouds dashing over the desert, and every-thing is so green. All the Navajos are back in the vicinity, not on the monument, but close, and every day representa-tives of the various families come to visit and spend several hours. It is nice to have them around again, although the preliminaries take up a terrific amount of time. . . .

At least [the visitors] won't be whizzing through this lit-tle monument very fast—our roads are simply terrible, at least 100% worse than when you were here, Liz. But don't tell anyone. About five cars a day seem to manage to get in. I surely hope they come—there is more to see to the square mile here than anyplace in the world. Did you know that to see all the kinds of country you see from the top of the Peaks, to the bottom of the Grand Canyon, you would have to drive 18,000 miles along the coast? . . .

Wupatki
August 9, 1940

Dear Gagoo and Aunt Clara,

. . . This is starting out to be such a busy month, that I hadn't realized it was August yet. We are having more visitors than ever before. Davy and the CCC boy have parties going around the ruin almost all the time, and I often have to take a few until one of them is free. This morning I was typing and had the front door open and a lady came up the ladder and called for me by name and asked if she and her family could come in—they had seen one of our articles, and just had to see the house. . . . Sometimes it is a bit annoying to have lots of people coming to look at the

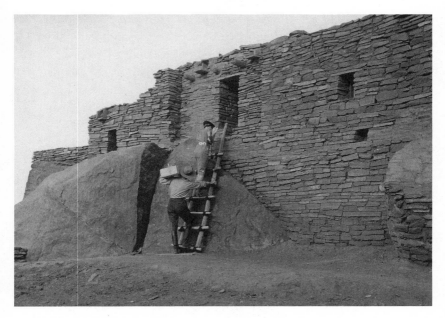

Davy and Courtney climbing the ladder to their apartment in the Wupatki ruin (Photograph by Tad Nichols)

house, but we really enjoy meeting some of them, and I know they get such a kick out of it. It won't be long until we are out of the ruin, and then I think some of our visitors will really miss something interesting.

Last Friday Davy had to give a talk in town. The Arizona Highway Commission put on a little program for the local people. . . . and Davy was to show a movie on the national monuments, but the movie didn't come, so he showed his slides of Wupatki and really made a grand talk. This Friday they have asked him to repeat it at Kingman. . . . I'm glad he is doing so well in this line as it will mean more trips around the country for us, and we do love to go places and see things.

We are quite certain now that they won't finish our house before the end of September. They are paving the patio now, and it is going to be very pretty, and quite easy to take care of. I'm disappointed not to have a tree in it, but they may be able to put one in later. Right now there will be flagstones in the center, and walks to the various doors, with grass between the stones. Then there are four strips to be planted with flowers along the four walls. They will have to be something which can stand a lot of heat and sun, so I'm counting on rows of nasturtiums and zinnias. We have a lovely little wild zinnia here, about four inches high and loaded with yellow flowers with large orange centers. . . .

We went over to visit the Navajos last Saturday. Several people brought in presents for them and we took them over. We only had a general idea of where they were living, so it was a thrilling excursion. We took a picnic supper, and ate it in the middle of the grassland while the truck stopped boiling—we had to go about three or four miles cross-country, as there was no road. It was fun to see them all again. The baby is so big now, and runs around and is starting to talk. I think he remembered us, because he shook hands with us like he used to. . . .

Wupatki
September 1940

Dear M.,

We've been wondering how you weathered the FLOOD. It sounded awful on the other side of the mountains [in Tucson] and aren't you glad you don't have electricity—or do you?? I have the vaguest impression of your present *casa*—can remember a corral, and you've mentioned curtains, a bathtub and a cow. . . .

Davy is starting to brace up the crumbling ruins—has Wukoki, the watch tower, to fix first and it will take a couple of months. [It took a couple of years.] But I still say it's the prettiest ruin in the Southwest and it deserves help.

We have a boarder!! Pretty good for 40 miles from town, isn't it? He is the nicest elderly man, a retired engineer whose great dream is to develop a preservative which will make it possible to take the roof off of Casa Grande. He has acres of experiments here and his untreated 'dobes vanished in the last rain—the others are still here, so he's making headway. It is much fun to have him as he works like a beaver and is full of enthusiasm. Surely puts an incentive into meal planning and we are eating like elephants. Buchenburg is the name. Incidentally, he pays me $7.50 a week.[19]

It is simply wonderful here now, what with the rains. Grass all over the place and the Navajos camped all around the boundaries, waiting to spring across the minute it has seeded. . . .

Wupatki
late September 1940

Dear Lizzie B.,

. . . Mr. B. is still with us and we like him a lot. We got
to noticing about a week ago that when we could see him
coming over to meals in his little old coupe he would be
just barely moving along, down by the ballcourt[20]—then
he would start up with a roar and tear up the hill. After
several days of this, Davy asked him about it and he said
he was seeing how far he could coast from the hill by his
cabin. "Oh, my," he said, "You should see me skid around
the corner and thru the gate—I hate to put on the brake as
it slows me too much." He also figured he could coast farther on a hot day. He is full of little experiments like that,
in fact, his life is a series of them. Davy tried the coasting
and can go to the cook shack that way, which beats Mr. B.,
although Mr. B. consoles himself with the theory that the
truck, being heavier, accounts for that. . . .

We went to see the Navajos one day and Mr. B. was delighted. Sally fed us some kind of melon which tasted like
sweet cucumber, and she cut it in little dainty strips. Grandmother Peshlakai was there (age 93), and Ruby and Gladys,
her granddaughters. They were having a Sing[21] for Gladys,
who apparently has TB. She and Ruby spin better than anyone else, and G. is a good weaver. Ruby is good, but not ar-
tistic. Mr. B. carried Charley Clyde around all the time, wet
pants and all. Sally made the prettiest rug we ever saw and
was going to enter it in the Window Rock Fair, but was too
late. We will buy it for the new house, and enter it next year.

The Cravens[22] from New York . . . asked Mr. B. and us
to the Grand Canyon for dinner Sunday. Pretty slick, so we
could use his car, see. Well, that is fine, except for the 91-
mile drive late at night. . . . Davy drove so there was no
experimental coasting, and it was a lovely ride. It got to

pouring up there and there were *drifts* of hail along the road. But just at sunset the sky glowed red, and we came to a break in the trees. The Canyon was full of purple mist and the edge of each cliff was bright red. It was magnificent! Then we had dinner—shrimp cocktail, chicken soup, salad with Roquefort dressing, fried scallops, roast turkey, sweet and white potatoes, fresh peas, hard rolls, and ice cream. Each thing separate except the main course. Then they showed color slides—their home in Mountain Lakes, New Jersey; Zuni and Taos pueblos; Wupatki; the World's Fair at night. We started home at 10:45 and got here at 2:00. Got up at 6:00 as usual and had to go to town, so [we] are still in a stupor.

While we were away, a cloudburst hit Wupatki, and the road here was washed out so we could hardly get up. The floor was covered with water and is still wet in one place. The trail to the john was gone and a foot of dirt in front of its door had to be shovelled out. The ground on one side of the cook shack raised three feet, burying a woodpile.

I forgot to say that the Cravens gave us a beautiful oil painting (by Mr. Craven) of Wupatki.

As you could have guessed if I hadn't told you, the *house* is about the same as last June, since it hasn't been touched, except that it is getting dirty and the roof and walls leak. They are running a rock drill (what they break paving with) next to it for the museum, so T.G. we aren't in it— the noise is annoying.

Wupatki
November 2, 1940

Dear Twinsies,

. . . Our main event of the season was the pack trip, and I will try to tell you about it. We left here real early on a

Thursday morning, after rising at four. Went to town and got food for the trip and for the Brewers, got a lunch and started out. It is always a thrill to drive right past our entrance and on north on the highway. The weather was perfect, warm and sunny like Indian summer. At Tuba City we turned off to the Hopi village of Moencopi, to get some pumpkins for Jack-O'-Lanterns for a surprise party for Jimmy and Sallie. Then we hastened on, as we wanted to get there before dark, but the road was very bad—it is over 100 miles off the paving. You can see so far after crossing the Painted Desert—the Peaks at Flagstaff; Navajo Mountain, which Rainbow Bridge is behind; Wild Horse Mesa; White Mesa, which looks like chalk; the Echo Cliffs which are brilliant red; and all sorts of strange formations. The whole country is flat with these mesas sticking up, and it is covered with sage, which, Liz will remember, is sort of dull blue, and lots of juniper and pinyon trees. We got there [Navajo National Monument] just as the sun went down, and their house is just darling. It is right in thick trees, and built out of blue-gray stone, so it looks like a playhouse, sort of hidden. They have a kitchen, living room, of which one wall is a fireplace, and a bedroom and bath. Davy and I had a hogan they have fixed up for guests, and Mr. B. slept on the davenport. They have lots of Navajo rugs, in soft colors, and Jimmy has made all the furniture, which is plain natural wood and just lovely.

The next morning they had planned a trip to Inscription House Ruin, which is said to have had a Spanish name and date on one of the walls, but only the date is still there. It was a long drive, 20 miles, on top of the mesas, and then a three-mile walk down into a red rock canyon, and along a little running stream to the ruin. The canyon is full of ruins, many of which haven't been explored. The main ruin is part way up a sheer cliff, in a rounded cave. To get to it you have to climb up the straight face of the cliff with little toe-holds scooped out of the rock—fine if you keep going real fast but terrible if you stop, as you can't really support your weight in them. It was the cutest ruin I ever saw, and I mean it. It is just like a miniature. The rooms are real tiny, and the doorways into the store rooms are so small that they must have only sent the kids into them—we couldn't get in. It is just as if the people had just left—the roofs are all on, and the beams and reeds are just like new except where they are smoked up. There are little shelves in the rooms, corner ones, and some clear across one side; ashes in the firepits, and little dried corn cobs and pieces of gourd and melon rinds scattered on the slope below. It was real hot in the cave as all the ruins in the country up there are built in caves that the sun shines in almost all day in the winter, and the rocks get hot and reflect the heat.

On the way back Sallie and I took off our shoes and waded up the stream to where you climb out of the canyon. There were several Navajo families camped along it and they were harvesting their corn. One man was sitting in a tent made out of blankets. He had a pile of corn in front of him on a blanket and was beating it with a stick to loosen the grains so they could get them off the cobs easily. He said Davy could take his picture for a dollar, so we didn't. There he was with long hair, and probably hardly ever saw white people but he had heard of how to make money that way.

One of the things we had most counted on up there was to be able to take baths in their bathtub. Well, their pump doesn't work, it filled the tank once and has never worked since, so they were about out of water and we even felt wasteful flushing the john. So the next day Davy and Jimmy were going to try to fix the pump. Jimmy went

Courtney showering near the cook shack. This shower was used only a couple of times. (Photograph by Mary Jane Nichols)

down into the canyon and then Davy and Mr. B. and I went down. Mr. B. was just thrilled to see Betatakin, although he couldn't manage to climb up into it. We had a picnic lunch with Jimmy and then went up to start the pump motor. It still didn't work, so Jimmy said he would give up for the time being and go on the pack trip.

The next morning, Pipeline, the Clyde of that monument, arrived with the pack mules and extra horses. I didn't feel good, so Sallie and I stayed home and the boys and Pipeline went on to make the main camp and see one ruin. The next morning Sallie and I started out, and it is just amazing where those horses can walk. Right up and down smooth sandstone rocks, and jump off places where there is no trail, and I would certainly rather be on one than walking. Pipeline met us just where the trail started to get really bad—he was just rare all the time—helping us along like we were children, and telling us about the country. Liz may remember him coming in the tent when we were up at Betatakin—he doesn't talk much English, but is very entertaining. He called me *"Aht-zahn Sozhie,"* which means Slim Woman.

The base camp was in a lovely spot, a wide flat valley with red cliffs on both sides, and the Tsegi River in a little canyon in the middle. There were several old hogans, falling into ruins, and a little shade, which was three trees with the tops sort of interlaced, with a cleared floor and a little wall of logs around it. It was just big enough for our bedrolls and a little fire in the middle. The wall was just high enough to wash dishes on.

After we had eaten lunch we all went up Bubbling Spring Canyon—a narrow canyon, which had filled up with sand dunes about half way, and the little spring flows all the time and has cut a little canyon. We saw a horse that had gotten caught in the quicksand and died. The spring really bubbles up out of the ground and we all drank some. Up where the canyon was wider there were three caves in a row with ruins in all. There were lots of oaks turning red and yellow, and it was just beautiful, but the ruins weren't very big or well-preserved.

Pipeline didn't go in the ruins because Navajos don't like them on account of the ghosts, so he went to visit some friends who had a hogan nearby. While he was there he had some fresh roasted horsemeat—they don't eat it very often. Then we started "home" (base camp) to get there before it got too dark and cold as we had no lamps. It was fun to sit around the fire and talk, and Jimmy was rare as usual, and Pipeline told us stories about the canyons and how they all had lakes when he was a child, but it got real cold so we went to bed. We all got undressed and into our sleeping bags, and had quite a time getting all settled, but Pipeline just took all the horse blankets and laid down and put a blanket over himself, and we envied him because he was just as comfortable with no trouble at all.

For supper we had Navajo fried bread, which Sallie knew how to make—flour, baking powder, and water, mixed stiff and patted out into thin cakes and fried in deep bacon grease—the Navajos use mutton fat. It gets all brown and bubbly and is quite good when you have nothing better.

The next morning we were all stiff, and Jimmy was worrying about the water supply at Betatakin, so decided to stay out just that one day. In the morning we went to Scaffold House, about three miles from our camp. . . . Then we went back and had lunch and started back to the house, after packing the mules. They were little bitty creatures, and the packs were bigger than they—all the bedrolls and food, but they would just run along ahead faster than we could go. There is about a two-hundred-foot sand dune to go up before you are on the trail, which is cut out of the cliff, so you can imagine what a climb it is. It is terrific to hang onto the horse when it is jumping up those big boulders. But as I said before, I'd rather be doing that than trying to climb. . . .

We stayed another day and night, and Jimmy and Davy went down and worked on the pump again, and Mr. B. figured out the engineering on it, and they got it to pump for about half an hour, then gave up. We left the next morning, still without getting a real bath, but it was a grand trip anyway. We got here just in time, as the next day it clouded up and rained half an inch here, and snowed in town. We went to town three times in the next five days, as Davy is working on a report, so don't feel quite settled yet.

Mr. B. got off all right I guess, and we had dinner with him in town the night before he left. He will be back in the spring, as he is planning to finance some badly needed work around this ruin. Now Davy has a lot of terrific reports to get out and then we hope to get at our furniture.

Yesterday one of our visities went over to paint a picture of Sally weaving, and we took the other man to see some little cliff dwellings in one of the canyons that Clyde showed Davy not long ago. Nobody knew anything about them and they are different from anything we have heard about, so Davy took some pictures and may write them up. The man who did the painting offered to come back sometime and help with Museum work here for his board—so if he does, I will certainly be running quite a little boarding house. And people have the nerve to ask how we can stand being so lonely clear out here. . . .

Wupatki
November 20, 1940

Dear Twinsies,

. . . Mr. Gordon Vivian, the ruin stabilizer, came Tuesday. He stayed at the CCC camp and worked like the dickens and the first part of fixing up the big high wall is done, the most dangerous part. Now they just have to wait for the concrete to harden, so he has gone home. We had Thanksgiving last Thursday and had him over to dinner. I had a time fixing it, and then forgot to put the cranberry sauce on. But I roasted a chicken—the biggest thing that has been in our oven. The stuffing was funny but I will know how better next time. And wild rice and plum pudding. . . .

Some fun, we went out in the evening and it was snowing. In fact when we opened the door it had drifted against it about two inches. Davy has to keep flares going up on

Sally Peshlakai (Photograph by Rex Fleming)

the top of the ruin to keep the concrete from freezing and he had a time with them that night. And it was still snowing when we went to bed so we decided to get up early and get the mail so we could see the snow before it melted. Well, it is still on the ground. Imagine. And the visitors say we have lots more than Flagstaff, which is unheard of. In the morning it was six inches on the level, and drifted to your knees in places. Very treacherous walking because the dang little rocks were all covered and you couldn't tell where to step. We put on boots, and Davy wore my earmuffs, and I wore my new hat, which is a boy's hunting cap of blue plaid corduroy with ear flaps, and we were all bundled up and having snow fights and taking pictures. We had to make the road all the way to the highway until a few miles in we met a CCC truck coming in. We would get a run for the hills, and stop in the drifts, and back down and get another run and so on. It took us an hour and a half to get there in low, instead of twenty minutes as usual. And is it pretty. The sky was white like the ground.

When we came back we drove over to Clyde's by a roundabout road as he was away and we were afraid Catherine and Grandmother didn't have enough wood. But he came in on horseback just after we did. Sally came home in the wagon later—they had all been to Cameron to a Sing. It doesn't feel very cold, and [the snow] melts a bit in the daytime and is sure fun to play out in. Davy had to shovel off all the roofs in the ruin. Today the sky was turquoise blue and the desert is white, and the rocks are dark red because they are wet, and there were little birds singing and hunting around in the bushes. Tonight I went out with Davy to light the flares, and the starlight is like daylight almost on the snow. . . .

I forgot to tell you that Jean McWhirt and Addison Pinkley (the Boss's son) were married Sunday, the tenth. They will live at Parker Dam, California—a big new dam that Addison is working on. He is an engineer. . . .

Wupatki
December 1940

Dear M.,

. . . Now where is this Kelley Place, and will you be on it or in it soon again? Southern Arizona seems to get farther and farther away from here, but sometime in the future the truck has to be overhauled at Coolidge, or we will be hitchhiking to town, and so we hope for a sight of a saguaro again this winter. And they hope to have another

Southwestern Monuments Conference in February, so at least we will get down to it. We had planned to go [visit Davy's folks in Gallup] . . . for Christmas, but there is no one to look after the monument. . . . As it stands we have Christmas here with the Navajos and then will try to get over to Gallup, if it is possible, for a few days.

We are still in the ruin, which could use a bit of weatherstripping at present—and you can't imagine the place covered with snow, yes, SNOW. It is simply elegant, and is something not to be missed, so for your information, Clyde says, "Next full moon coming, little bit snow, maybe lots snow"—can you make it? . . .

Did you know we had a boarder for over two months? And with what success. This nice man went to Casa Grande and wanted to do some experiments, it being his dream to remove the roof from that ruin—pretty good goal, isn't it. Well, he is a retired engineer, and very nice, but didn't get along in the heat of summer there, so they sent him up here. Well, he arrived just like any visitor and he and Davy took to each other and before two visits were over he was ready to finance an exhibit of a rubbish section in place. So he moved out to the Forest Service cabin (no goat stable for him) and started whizzing around whipping up little miniature exhibits and busy as a beaver, and boarding here and no trouble at all. He would never stay in the house, just came in on the dot for meals, and we just loved him—very interesting man. So it came time to migrate southways, when the bitter winds began seeking out all the cracks in the cabin, and in parting, he decided to give Wupatki $1,000 for further cleaning up and research—it is all on paper now, with the stipulation that Davy have complete charge, but not finally accepted through the red tape, etc. So he will be back in the spring, we think. . . .

Clyde Peshlakai (Photograph by Rex Fleming)

Wupatki
January 8, 1941

Dear Lizzy Begay,

. . . This is the funniest Christmas I have ever put in, and it was fun but not like what I have been brought up on. We were down with colds before so everything was a mess. We planned to go to Gallup the day after Christmas so knew we would be rushed. So the Eve we opened our gifties and sort of celebrated but it was so funny without a tree, and besides it was pouring rain as it had been for three days, so we just piled in the truck and took off for Gray Mountain Trading Post. I guess that wasn't built when you were here. It is about fifteen miles down the highway toward Cameron. We like the Reids who run it, and it was fun to spend the rest of the evening with a big family before a roaring fireplace with a big Christmas tree.

It poured so hard and was snowing in toward the mountain and they wanted us to stay all night, but we had so much planned for the next day that we came home. The roads were like rivers—you just can't imagine the precipitation. Well Christmas day dawned bright and clear—the only clear day for weeks, but blowing fit to bust. We took off after breakfast to distribute things to the Navajos, and was it fun. The little kids were just darling with their things. Charley Clyde is so smart you just can't believe it. We gave him a humming top that you sort of pump, and Davy ran it for him. When it stopped, Clyde picked it up and thought you had to wind it, so he couldn't work it, so Davy showed him again. Then little Charley Clyde grabbed it and pumped it and he could run it all by himself. We sure tease Clyde about it but he doesn't think it is very funny.

Hal's[23] family's hogan just has no roof at all and we thought how miserable they will be, but when we got inside it was cozy as anything, and the sun streaming in and a little fire going, and then you would look up and there would be the sky and the wind. I can't understand it. Grandmother is living with them now, but Hal wasn't there—visiting his other wife I guess—he will be sorry, as we gave them five pounds of candy. Imagine five pounds of chocolates for 80 cents. They were good too. We gave grandmother cigarettes—isn't that a rare thing for an old lady, 95 years old, but that is what she wanted. It took all morning, and we couldn't get to Grandpost's,[24] but it was just like being home with all the family on Christmas, in a way.

Then we tore home and cleaned house and put away all

Catherine Peshlakai and her children Richard and Eleanor at a
hogan, 1958 (Photograph by Zorro Bradley, courtesy of Wupatki
National Monument)

our things and started the chicken, as Dorothy and Al
Whiting[25] and their baby Eric, and Gertrude Hill from the
library were coming out for dinner at noon. They didn't
come for ages, and we were real worried as we were afraid
they were snowed in; but finally in they rushed, with their
Christmas tree, and we set it up and decorated it and Dorothy decorated all the beams with tinsel. We had gathered
a lot of juniper mistletoe which looks like juniper with
pink berries and had planned a wreath for the door but it
was blowing too hard to put it out. Anyway it was really a

fun day and Eric was the center of attraction, especially
when he would pick up his jello and squeeze it through his
fingers. . . . After they left we packed our two new
suitcases—we got one for each other and Davy got me
one to match. . . .

We came home [from Gallup] on the bus Sunday night,
and stayed in Flag. The ranger didn't get in with the truck
till afternoon and it was pouring and sleeting and snowing
all day. So when we got home the ruin was leaking and we
were surrounded with mud and would have had to make
several trips to the cook shack, and then we were supposed
to go to Coolidge on the first and were invited to a dance
the night before and only one day to do all that we had to,
so we just left the suitcases packed and went to town and
stayed all night. . . . The next morning we went off for
Coolidge. It was snowing lovely fluffy snow and they had
the roads clear, and it quit snowing by the time we got to
Prescott. . . .

Phoenix and around there was a sight as they were having terrible floods. But it was warm though simply pouring,
and smelled heavenly. We went to Vahki [Inn] and cleaned
up and ate and went over to the monument [Casa Grande]
and everyone was having dinner at Chris and Hugh's [Mil-
ler] and were about to go to the show so they took us and
then we all sat around and visited until New Year's. We
were down there two days and had a lovely time feasting
and sitting around. Had to leave the truck there to be overhauled and you should see what we are driving around. We
were afraid it wouldn't get us home. It is the old truck
Jimmy Brewer had [bought by the Park Service for five
dollars] and sounds like it had chains on. . . .

The last night we went up to Phoenix to have a good rest
and head start, and the hotel where we stayed had a real
good orchestra so we got dressed up and went down and

danced—yes us, the first time since we were married. Glad
we got some practice as we are invited to the President's
Ball. That night we stayed in Prescott. And the next day
came home by way of Jerome, the town on the hill, and
Oak Creek. It is still rainy and gloomy as there are thick
fogs all the time. But we have gotten things pretty well
straightened up and are full of good New Year's resolutions.

Well, this may be all real boring, but it is the news from
around here and was very exciting while it was going on.
The wildest week I have put in. Davy is sharpening all our
knives tonight, so I will cut off a few fingers tomorrow.
Hope I get a few notes written first. We are full of new
ideas of things to make for Sunset and here this winter, so
will be quite busy from now on.

Wupatki
March 1941

Dear Lizzie Begay,

. . . The conference is over and Mr. B. is back, and the
work on the ruin is about to begin, and by golly, I think we
are going to MOVE! The conference in Coolidge was
grand. The meetings are so inspiring, with all the custodians there, and it is so good to see everyone that we have
been reading about. The Brewers got out all right. . . .
I guess they had a good winter although snowed in. . . .

I had terrible laryngitis and had to stay in bed one day,
but Davy went to Nogales and got our glassware and the
dining room chairs, which are unfinished wood with
rawhide seats—eight for ten dollars! . . .

A week ago Mr. B. arrived, only a month before we expected him, but it is nice to have him, although I am not
getting much done besides cooking. He had his trailer,
which is a trailer to end all trailers, sent up, and it is parked

in the canyon below the john. He has a john that flushes, lights, and all the fixings. The $1,000 was accepted of course and there will be all sorts of activity here this summer, with all the archaeologists coming in and whatnot. And the man who does all the research on ruins stabilization in Washington may set up a laboratory here this summer, which certainly puts Wupatki on the map. It is really going to be very important and will do Davy more good than going to Yale. . . .

It surely is an early spring out here and you would love to see it. . . . The grass is getting green here, and the loco is blooming—looks like perennial peas, purple and white—and the little low spring flowers are just starting to bloom and the rock wrens are singing just like canaries. I guess they haven't had a spring like this in years and years—it has rained every week for the whole winter. . . .

And they are working like mad on the house. We have ordered one set of chair cushions, and the CCC carpenter is going to cut the boards for us, then we will bring them out and put them together out here. In another week we should have one chair finished so we will know whether we want the other one like it. They are actually going to build me some good cabinets in the kitchen, and I am getting real excited about moving. . . .

Wupatki
April 21, 1941

Dear Lizzie Begay,

. . . Well, now we have been married three years and one day, and it doesn't seem like that long. The only difference is we don't have the big arguments so much anymore, having gotten things settled to both of our satisfaction long ago. . . .

Friday before Easter this clerk for the job here, who is
hired under the title of "roustabout," arrived. He is a nice
boy from Chicago, called Philip van Cleave[26]. . . . Phil
stays in the Forest Service cabin and . . . eats at the CCC
camp. . . . He tells us the bright sayings of the CCC boys,
which are rare. They are trying to make him think they are
a bunch of toughs, which some of them are . . . one of
them couldn't get his combination padlock open so one of
the others offered to pick it for him. He was twisting it
around and listening to it, and wondering whether he
shouldn't sandpaper his fingers, and he said to Phil, "See
that fly down at the end of the barracks on the bed?" and
Phil said yes, and then he said, "Well, I can't see it but I can
hear it walking around."

The dig started last Thursday and they ran right into a
sort of shelter with some painted sticks on the floor. They
are delicate and Davy spent about a half hour taking them
out with a little brush. This annoyed the boys who want
action, arrow points and burials. The dig consists of running trenches as deep as the original ground level from the
canyon up to the outer walls of the ruin, just to get the outline. They save the sherds [and] sift all the dirt through a
big rocker with five sizes of screen. They also save the scorpions alive and Phil has brought up two this afternoon. . . .

It is almost time to get supper. Dang, I have to start
about four o'clock. My time is surely spent "on the
range"—I get up at 6:00, have breakfast at 7:00, clean
house and do dishes, and make bread if necessary. Then it
is around ten and time to get lunch, which is at eleven.
Then I make some dessert or a salad, and before I know it
it's four and time to get supper. In the evenings I have been
knitting a Red Cross sweater while reading, and have finished it and am on one for myself. I also keep the bird and
flower notes, paying special attention to finding out

whether the wrens are starting to build. We have a flower blooming calendar to check when the different ones are in bloom, full bloom, or seed. Also, there are a lot of little annuals that we didn't know, and I have a stake by each of fifteen kinds on the way to the john and keep notes on their progress. . . .

We will not move till after the next fiscal year, July. The venetian blinds can't be bought till there are more appropriations, and wouldn't it be fun to live in a government house with the visities peeking in the windows. Rudi Egermeyer had a funny experience. A woman started peeking in her window [at Saguaro National Monument] while she was washing, or bathing, as we call it, in a basin. She went over and pulled the shade down in the woman's face, and the woman went to the next window and Rudi pulled down THAT shade, and so on around the whole house. Then she tried to get in the door, and Rudi told her she couldn't come in and she said, "Well, it's a government house, isn't it?" and Rudi said yes but we rent it and it's private, and the woman started to come in anyway. There was another woman with her who pulled her back and said, "Well, you bold thing, keep out of that house," and they started to fight, and began to pull out each other's hair, and Don had to come up and pull them apart. . . .

Wupatki
June 16, 1941

Dear Lizzie Begay,

. . . Did the folks send my letter about my trip with M. and Sarah Hubert and this boy Frank Fahey? [They were taking Jean McWhirt Pinkley up to her job as ranger at Mesa Verde.] If I had known how long we would be gone, I wouldn't have gone with them, as it left Davy here cook-

ing for Mr. B. and managing his dig and guiding and having a heck of a time, but it surely was wonderful and
hardly seems possible that we could see so much in such a
short time. . . . You would have loved seeing all the places,
and it was fun to cook our own food and sleep out the two
times that it didn't rain.

Mesa Verde, where we got the first day, is different from
what I had expected in a way. You drive along the base of
the big mesa along a river, with little farms on each side
and it is just like the East, I suppose, in that there are lots
of trees, and all very green, and lilacs and honeysuckle in
all the yards. Then you go up on the mesa by the most
hair-raising road that clings to the edge of cliffs with sheer
walls going up on one side and down on the other. The
views are grand. Then on top are forests of juniper and
pines and millions of wildflowers, including wild forget-
me-nots and wild plum bushes. The edge of the mesa is all
cut into by little canyons with sheer walls, and in caves in
them are the ruins. The ruins are none of them as pretty or
spectacular as Betatakin, but they are huge affairs, and
since they are just over the top and far above the bottom
of the canyon, you go over the top and climb down to
them, partly on paths and partly on ladders.

It was the first time I had been on caravan trips with a
ranger. All the cars line up and he goes in the first one, and
then you all get out and he gives you talks at each place. It
is so arranged that you get out above one ruin, climb down
to it and then continue around the cliff at the same level to
the next ruin, and so on for about three hours and then
you climb up. Balcony House is the last one you go to in
the afternoon and they keep trying to discourage all the
ones who have a hard time climbing before they get there,
as you have to go up a thirty-foot ladder. It is a darling
ruin, with a little balcony on the front wall, like a little

porch with two little doors opening out on it. In the back
of the cave is a good spring and they let you drink out of
it. All the ruins are very neat and clean, and look fresh and
new, except that scarcely any of the rooms have roofs, so it
isn't as thrilling as Betatakin.

Jean McWhirt Pinkley lives in the hospital; she is the
only girl ranger. In her room is a gruesome thing that they
keep handy in case anyone falls off a cliff—a wire basket
in the shape of a person so that if he were still in one piece
he could be strapped into it, and then it has runners so it
could be pulled straight up. Fortunately it hasn't been used
but I would hate to have it staring me in the face every
morning. Jean did fall off a ladder and caught her leg in a
rung and fainted, but they got her up before they got the
basket there. . . .

Well, we were there a full day and part of the next, and
would have loved to stay longer but by that time they had
decided to take the long way home through Colorado and
Utah. All the trip was fine and fun as M. was real rare and
Sarah is full of lots of bright remarks, and Frank is very
nice although sort of spoiled rich boy type, who thinks
you don't have to obey the speed laws in the little towns
and doesn't know that you can't drive lickety-cut through a
herd of sheep.

While I was away Davy got the pieces of the living
room chair glued and doweled together and since then we
have finished one! All but putting on the woodfiller and
varnish. And is it comfortable—oh, my. It is just like a
cloud, and here we had been so worried for fear it would
be hard or the wrong slant on the cushions or something.
So we have cut out the pattern for the other one just like
it, and then will get it and the davenport cut out tomorrow,
and before you know it, it will be all done. It takes a lot of
work, in rasping and filing and sanding the edges so they

are round and smooth. We worked two hours a night for two weeks on that one but it won't take so long for the others, now that we know how. Every afternoon I go over for at least an hour and sandpaper the little Mexican dining room chairs, so before we move in maybe they will be finished too. We think we'll be moving in July, and I really can hardly wait. Of course the house won't be all furnished for a long time and maybe the things will look bare without the little end tables that make the arms of the davenport and so on, but with all the Navajo rugs we have, it will cover up some of the bare spots. . . .

All of this furniture stuff keeps us busy all the time in our "spare" moments, besides which the grass, which is very spotty and weak, has to be watered as well as the shrubs and my little nasturtiums. I also planted more seeds of marigolds, forget-me-nots, bachelor buttons and zinnias since I came home. Our lettuce border supplied salads and I have planted another border of it, which should be going good by the time we are over there. The mockingbirds were a riot last week singing constantly all day—one of the darn fools was flying over the Forest Cabin while I was washing, pretending he was a flock of pinyon jays calling to beat the band. And then there is a family of little wrens around and the mother calls to them and scolds them, and the mockingbird would mock her all the time. Last night I saw a hummingbird, too. . . .

Wupatki
July 1941

Dear M.—

Oh joy, oh rapture unconfined! The magnificent and gorgeous and wonderful radio is here—and M., it is just perfect and we are so delighted to have it, really. It is going to be marvellous to be able to hear good music. . . . You are a swell gal to send it, and it's going to give us a lot of fun and entertainment.

Saw Gertrude Hill at the opening of the Hopi Craftsman[27]. . . and she said you were off for the East. To our great disappointment, but we'll be seeing you in the fall or winter when you migrate back to the open spaces again. . . .

Time speeds along at a breathtaking rate and what all has happened since *the trip* is simply phenomenal. We have moved practically everything but ourselves into the house and are sanding and rasping on furniture like mad every evening. Then yesterday was a day we have been awaiting with dread for some time—our radio debut was to take place in Prescott, besides which the regular getting of supplies had to be done, and it was the opening of the Craftsman, which is the main event of the year to us in these parts. So we went in the night before and were up till all hours rehearsing and cutting the script with a friend who has just moved here and knows how it's done. Got in to see just a tantalizing glimpse of all the dazzling array of baskets, rugs and whatnot, then off to Prescott with this Dorothy Farrar who was going to do the interviewing of the famous ranger from Wupatki. Good thing we got an early start, for the road was about 90 percent under construction, and we were panting when we steamed up to the studio. Kept waiting for the much-overrated "mike fright," which never reared its ugly head, and the whole thing went off with aplomb or whatever you'd call it. Guess we never had time to get excited; and then we found that the station covers a range of thirty-five miles! Haven't found anyone YET that heard us, except the Auntie and Uncle, who were in the next room in the station! . . .

Mrs. Colton isn't well, and is going to the coast for the rest of the summer. She doesn't have anyone to stay with

her for the first two weeks, beginning July 10th, so she
asked me to go along. They've been swell to us and really
it will mean a grand vacation and rest. Apparently all I
have to do is cook, and the rest of the time just sit or sleep,
which sounds too too heavenly after our summer in this so-
called isolation. It happens, fortunately, that my conscience
is more than clear with regard to the poor overworked husband and boarder, for about ten men are going to be here
grappling with the crumbling ruins and setting them to
rights, and all will be eating at the camp. They of course
insist most kindly that they would have more fun and
chances to argue if they ate with all the rest of the crowd,
so I'm going to take them at their word. . . .

By the way, Mrs. C. has an apartment at Laguna Beach, a
block from the ocean, which I've only seen once, and they
say it's most picturesque, being an artist's colony, and lots
of fascinating shops, so I don't exactly shun the trip.

Wupatki
September 1941

Dear Lizzie Begay,

. . . You should see me in my bubble bath! Remember?
You gave the lovely stuff to me for my birthday last year
and I saved it hopefully to christen the tub with. It is deli-
cious and I'm still so thrilled at being able to bathe in a tub
that I take simply ages at it, soaking and playing with the
bubbles.

And we have one chair completely finished! It is a great
and inspiring sight, and I have to go in and sit in it every
day for a few minutes, although we really don't have time
to use the living room much. I put four coats of varnish on
it, and then waited a week and rubbed it till it was dull
with pumice and rotten stone, which took a day and a half.

The new house at Wupatki, 1941 (Photograph by Devereux Butcher)

But it is worth it. Davy . . . works outside all day and then works on the regular reports and stuff in the evenings. The outside work has been wonderful for him and he looks so tanned and husky, but we are both thrilled to have fall coming when we can let down a little and do stuff to the house and get things better organized.

Really, we had no idea it would mean so much to us to live in a real house. It is just wonderful to be here, and so sort of peaceful not to have to be all shut up in that tiny space and not know where anything was when we wanted it, and to have the office right in the living room, and to eat in the kitchen. This is all sunny and spacious and lovely. Davy uses one of the bedrooms for an office and no one can disturb him and he doesn't have to keep it

straightened up all the time. I feel about a hundred years
younger now. It is fun to whisk a dust mop over the floors
and have a clean house. Also I don't dread going to town
so much as we don't have to put away all the stuff [in the
cook shack] when we are so tired, and there is the sink to
wash the lettuce and stuff in. Oh joy. . . .

Wupatki
October 1941

Dear Lizzy Begay,
    . . . We are really getting a lot done around here. . . .
Last week I got excited about all the dead bushes in the patio and went out with my little shovel and had them all out
in a jiffy, besides transplanting the living bushes so that
there would be room for the wild ones we will put in. So it
looks real neat in the back patio. . . . Some boys will work
on it this afternoon and I think it will be ready to plant this
week. We still have weekly rains, and all the wildflowers
are blooming again and it is just keen to get out and work
on the yard. . . . We took some pictures of the house and
will send them to the folks and they can send them to
you. . . .
    . . . Davy brought Dr. Colton out here over the pro-
posed road from Sunset, to look for any ruins that might
need to be protected. They came cross-country and it took
them nearly all day and they said it was just magnificent.
Good views of the desert all the way and much more sce-
nic than the old road. I stayed at Coltons' and went walking with Mrs. C. and the dogs and went to her studio,
which is a little house with a fireplace on the edge of a little canyon, and watched her carve wood—she is making
the head of a Hopi girl. . . . We came [home] by a road
that goes through low cinder hills and they were lovely—

Wukoki's leaning wall being repaired, 1941 (Photograph by
David J. Jones)

the big rabbit brush was clumps of orange and there were
red [lemonade sumac] bushes all along the slopes, so it was
really grand fall color for this country.

We have had Al Whiting, the ethnobotanist [*Ethnobotany
of the Hopi*], here working on the stuff from the ruin—he
identified the beans and stuff, and has been here a month.
Every Friday Dorothy, his wife, would come for him. I like
her a lot, she used to do that therapy work in hospitals,
teaching crafts, and is very interesting. They have a darling
baby, Eric, who is just starting to talk and tear around. . . .
His favorite sport is taking all the things out of the cupboards in the kitchen but he isn't destructive, and when
you can't walk through any longer you just tell him to put
them back and he does, actually remembers just where
everything goes. . . .

Mr. B. doesn't eat with us since I was in Laguna Beach, he eats at the camp and really I am quite glad. He has fun over there with the boys and I can work as long as I want and not have to plan food and keep making fancy dishes all the time.

We also have a construction man Mr. B. hired to fix up the ruins. He is very nice and lives in the Forest Cabin and does his own cooking. He is fixing the tall wall that was leaning so long and it really looks wonderful—just exactly as it has always looked with the rocks slanting and all, but it is all stuffed with concrete and will stand forever—we hope. Mr. B. is more interested in stabilizing the ruins than doing anything else now, and really it is a good thing, for by digging you just uncover more stuff that will fall if it isn't protected, so he will get everything stabilized before any more digging is done. It is good for Davy to have so much help, too. . . .

Wupatki
October 1941

Dear Folksies,

. . . We have weekly rains still and two toadlets have appeared in the patio, hopping round and round, splashing happily in the puddles and seeming much at home. Our pet lizard has disappeared, but maybe good weather for toads is the kind when lizards are curled up someplace warm. We had the fireplace going all yesterday afternoon and evening. . . . Clyde is going to cut wood for us in return for us hauling wood for him, so we will hope to lay in a good supply for the winter. He and many of the other Navajos have been putting in a pipeline for their sheep over below our spring. . . .

The magazine with the article about overgrazing just

Catherine and Sally Peshlakai shearing sheep (Photograph by David J. Jones)

came and we haven't read it yet, but it should be helpful. And we have had a stroke of luck—after worrying about the punk stock in here, we found from the Range Rider that the Navajo tribe owns good stock and any Navajos can borrow bucks to breed with their own ewes. They have to send their own bucks to a pasture the tribe keeps up where they will be herded and taken care of just for the wool from the shearing of them. This keeps them out of the way, and they have had wonderful luck at building up the stock of the people who borrow the good bucks. We thought it would be hard to persuade Clyde and the others in here to borrow some this fall, but Davy told them about it and they said, "We will take two, tell them to bring them

over any time"; so there is not going to be any trouble on
that score. If they get the stock built up, they will not need
so many sheep, for the wool crop alone will be greatly increased and bring in plenty of money from fewer sheep.

Wupatki
October 1941

Hi, M.!

You don't know what you've done for us with that
radio—well, it is simply part of our lives now, and I can't
imagine how we did without one. It is surely fun to work
to music as we try to finish up various pieces of furniture,
and also to sit in the furniture and listen and knit. Davy
likes to type to it but I'm not that good a concentrator.
Every time we have had something good lately I have
thought to whip you off a letter, a paean of joy, but always
am overcome by lethargy or something. Anyway we think
of you. . . .

Things just whip along here. Al Whiting . . . an ethnobotanist . . . has been here a month looking over the wonderful fragments of STUFF Davy found in the little storage
room—did I tell you he found a little storeroom that
hadn't ever been a bit moist and was simply stuffed with
cloth scraps, sandals, grass, corn, squash rinds, stems, and
seeds, and even cottonwood leaves that look as if they fell
last year? Well, Al has been going over that and helping
with the other work and we have had a fine time with him.
He left just as another Al arrived for the winter—Al
Schroeder. . . . He just got a master's in archaeology at the
University of Arizona and he is here to survey the ruins, all
of them, on the monument, and put them all on a map. It is
fun to hear archaeological discussions all the time. In the
Forest Service cabin is a construction man who is stabilizing

the walls—has the tall toppling one, Wukoki, still looking as if it would keel over every minute but hidden inside is lots of concrete and stuff so it will continue as is forever— we hope. It is no one-man monument anymore, at least while the work on the ruins continues.

The house is getting better all the time. The best thing will always be the sink as far as I'm concerned, but of course a bit of interior decorating and some furniture is a help. . . . Davy has the best taste that I have run across, and I just do what he says most of the time because he seems to KNOW what is needed. . . . Did I tell you that Father was here for a week? . . . He didn't want to go touring around, just sit in the sun and do whatever we were doing, so he would sit out in the patio in his shorts and work on the dining room chairs—got all but one finished, and that was something, but what was even more of a SOMETHING—he washed all the windows! Inside and out. It was simply dazzling, and I hope someday to wash them again, but maybe it would be better to wait until it stops raining or until we have some more company. Hint, hint. I worked along with Fath, so got another chair finished for the living room. Think I have most of the wedding presents unpacked and on shelves now and tomorrow we inaugurate, or baptize or whatever it is, the new good dishes. . . . How long does it take to get a house fixed up, anyway? I guess there is always something to be done— but we hope to be comfortable by Christmas and finished in a year—a good test of patience, but it is the most fun we've had and I don't know a better way to spend the time than working on something you are going to live in and with.

The aspens have passed their prime most places now, but are still very pretty, and we try to go to town by way of around the Peaks all the time. . . . Didn't know we had

Courtney and her father, George Reeder, sanding Mexican chairs in the courtyard of the new house, 1941 (Photograph by David J. Jones)

so much pretty fall color. Maybe it is just because we haven't seen maples and oaks and all that stuff like you have for so long—I can imagine the East is pretty nice this time of year. Guess we won't get to take our pack trip in the Tsegi [near Monument Valley] this fall—just don't seem to have any Indian summer—at least we think, here it is, and then it lasts about three days and we have rain again. They have snow in the high country, and I don't know how much fun it would be to be in that maze of canyons in a blizzard, and as you will remember, there aren't any cabins for those too cold and damp to want to sleep out on the ground in a sleeping bag. . . .

Yesterday Davy took some boys and an extra truck and they all went down to Spider Web Ranch and got loads of manure for the front lawn-to-be. He says you would think that a cattle ranch would be the place to go, but they sure had a time finding two truckloads—at least it is properly antique, and I imagine this coming week will see a lot of activity in the yard. We got permission to do all the landscaping ourselves and I won't tell you, or give it a build-up, as this is a little premature, but heaven permitting we will have something green to rest the eyes on next summer. Did you ever smell a daphne? It is just ambrosia personified, and we have five that lived through the summer— supposed to be rather delicate but they love it here and will be our only "exotics." When I am busy and tearing around and wondering how to stop and get the next meal, I just go and smell one of the daphnes and feel like a lord of creation or something. . . .

I would like to know what-all you do when at home— any projects? Is it fun to be civilized and wear a dress and stockings and heaven forbid—a hat? . . . I suppose people there [New York] talk about the war a lot, but it is still pretty far away as far as hearing about it out here goes. It is kind of nice to be smug and complacent while we can.

Wupatki
December 30, 1941

Dear Lizzie Begay,

Oh, Happy Day! What darling and precious things and wrappings from you. . . . Where to begin—Davy's folks couldn't come, so we invited the Whitings to come out with Eric, and Phil to move over here for the holidays while the CCC was in town, so I just let the house go

knowing what it would be like, and had fun getting ready
for Christmas. We got a lovely blue spruce from the Forest
Service, and when we set it up on the card table it came
exactly to the ceiling, so Olga's angel she made for us
looked as if it floated. And then the Coltons gave us gobs
of real Virginia holly so we decorated the house. . . .

The next day we got all ready and the Whitings got
here for supper. And they brought their new puppy, named
Puddles since it isn't housebroken, and the dog from the
CCC camp came over. We were watching Puddles carefully but Butch got excited and forgot himself on one of
Eric's presents. . . . After breakfast we all tore into the presents, and boy did Eric have fun, as did we all. Davy gave
me simply tons of presents although he had given me
range pants already—copper cream and sugar lined with
turquoise enamel, silver ring like a heavy wedding ring, red
wool shirt for my Western outfit, and cologne. . . .

We weren't ready to sit down [for dinner] till about four.
Just as Davy was carving the turkey in came Clyde and in
spite of him saying it wasn't the "best right" to eat in the
afternoon, but only at noon and night, he sat down with us
too, and we all stuffed like horses for a couple of hours.
Then we got the Whitings to stay all night again, and the
next day was more calm in a way, but I must say you would
have said the house looked "lived-in" and anyone else
would have asked, "What by?" because we were having to
practically wade through the rooms. Sally and Catherine
Peshlakai and Charley Clyde came over in the morning
and did the kids have a great time with all the toys. . . .

We all went out on a hike one afternoon and had a grand
time looking for ruins and pictographs in the cinder hills. . . .
The whole house is simply coated with tiny finger and paw
and nose prints but I simply am letting it go for awhile. . . .

Wupatki

January 1942

Dear M.,

    . . . We had two dogs here for the holiday, one of them housebroken—together with Phil van Cleave who helped Davy with the dig last summer, and Al and Dorothy Whiting . . . and their baby, Eric, aged two. Needless to say it was a real Christmas, one of the best and most exciting, to have lots of people around all chortling and having a fine time, and we all got to hang up our stockings on account of having a fireplace, and what with Eric's pull toys all playing xylophones and drums or quacking, it was truly merry.

    We had fun getting ready too—what with the Coltons giving us slews of real Virginia holly which we padded out with our juniper loaded with blue berries into a wreath to end all wreaths—it fills the space between the mantel and ceiling in the living room, and lots was left over for the doors and such. . . . And then the day before the day before Christmas we did have a time—I made cookies to be decorated in the evening, and just after supper we were invited to a Sing for Sally Peshlakai. So we gave up the cookies and Phil, Davy and I took off for the Navajos'. We sat around hopefully for what seemed like hours and about nine o'clock they decided to eat and then have the Sing. So we came home and the boys decorated like mad with colored icing, and I baked another batch, and back we went to Sally's. This time they were all ready and had a real good Sing. She was supposed to be cured of a cough—well, the climax came when the medicine man went around and SPIT (yes he did) medicine on the assembled multitude. She says her cough is better. We stayed till about one and Phil stayed till six in the morning.

    It has really turned loose and blanketed the country with snow of the most exquisite variety. I can't say that we were simply overjoyed with snow in the East (Nebraska), but out here it is cause for much celebration and fun; somehow it looks so weird all over the desert, and so sparkly in the sunshine, and it is usually such calm brisk weather. Well, it got started and golly it went right on for a couple of days as if it were the most natural thing in the world, and when it finished—maybe it hasn't yet—it was about eight inches here and a foot near the highway. And Frabjous Day—we were actually snowed out of Flag! Not that we would have wanted to go in, but on New Year's Day we went down to the Gray Mountain Trading Post to visit, and one of the snowplow drivers was in there getting warm by the fireplace and he said they couldn't keep the road clear up near the summit and you would have to follow the snowplows to get to town at all. So we felt just too too perfectly isolated.

Now listen—what is all this wistful despair in which you appear to be plunged? You most certainly must come back to the West—what on earth will your cow do without you, to say nothing of Buster?? And last but not least—US? Don't you think they need air raid wardens in Tucson just as badly as in New York? Or you could get away from it all and just help us get some furniture made. Maybe a few more weeks of wearing a hat that isn't ten-gallon size will wear you down. If it keeps on snowing we would like another hand for shovelling snow off the ruin roofs—it's quite a task.

Wupatki
February 1942

Dear M.,

This is being written to the accompaniment of the tune of a cement mixer—the CCC boys started pouring cement for the foundation of the administration building today and the rumor is that they will work in shifts until they get it done, far into the night if necessary. . . .

It is really thrilling to hear how well organized things are back there and I know it must be exciting gathering blood donations and such. We got all excited and wanted to help, but so far all we hear is that we may have a spotting station. Davy wanted to take the auxiliary police course, but they were giving it several times a week and they won't let us use so much gas so we can't go in often enough. We may cut down our trips to once every two weeks, which really would suit us fine. The Navajos will love it if we get to start watching airplanes—they are so interested and want to help all they can. They had a meeting up near The Gap and passed the hat for the Red Cross, netting 80 dollars, and then all voted to sell one sheep apiece and give the R.C. the money—to top that they said they wanted to buy defense bonds, and one of them bought $1500 worth. With the Hopis it is a different story—someone told them that they were related to the Japanese—so they try to evade the draft, and are being generally uncooperative.

We keep expecting snow or something, and all we get is simply delightful weather down here—although on a windy day it is something to watch the snow blowing off the tops of the Peaks—great plumes of it streaming off. We have been getting around the monument a lot lately—had Eddie McKee, the geologist who used to be the naturalist at the Grand Canyon, and now is the assistant director of the Museum, and Barbara and their three children out for the weekend, a week ago. The kids were the first people who have been glad our rugs slide on the floor—they would get down at one end of the living room and with whoops they would run like mad and slide to the other end—it was just wonderful and I was sorry I had never thought of it. I had all the food cooked before they got here, so we spent the entire time outdoors just covering territory, so Davy could show Eddie some of our remarkable formations—and did I get stiff climbing, now that I am out of practice, what with no ladder anymore. The littlest boy collects bones—any kind, but he is particularly interested in saber-toothed tigers; however, he would have the back of the truck filled with sheep skeletons every time we stopped. Barbara and Eddie let him take most of them home, too.

Just as they were leaving on Sunday, Sallie and Jimmy Brewer drove in to stay with us till Tuesday—and since they hadn't been in to visit since they left Wupatki for Navajo, we were really thrilled, and it was a good excuse for some more tours. We went down and crossed the river [the Little Colorado], which was flooding, and thrilling, and looked over the new dam the Indian Service is putting in. It is to give the Navajos floodwater for raising crops. They have a CCC camp, and many of the boys from these families are working there. The foreman invited us to lunch, and it was lots of fun. It is the neatest camp, and they have a much nicer kitchen than our CCC, and good food. The Navajo CCC *boys* range in age from about 15 to 70! Then we looked at the pictographs—did you ever see them? And drove on into the desert farther than any of us had ever been—and you would be surprised to see how much like Monument Valley it is, and the ground is just littered with petrified wood.

Did you know that a few weeks ago—guess I didn't write you about it—we went up on Black Point, the biggest mesa between here and Cameron, and far out on the end, over the river, was a Hopi shrine and part of the old Hopi trail which used to go from the villages to the salt mines in the Canyon. It really was a marvellous find, and people had known about the trail but had never found just where it was. We asked Clyde about it and he knows where a lot of it is and is going to take us on a pack trip to trace it. I'm glad we can do it as it will be a fine thing for Davy to write up—hope he is going to get time this winter to write up some of the things that are of interest to science around here, as it will do him good to appear in print occasionally. Anyway we are thinking it might be more fun to have Clyde take us in his wagon, rather than on horseback, and now can hardly wait for warm weather.

Last time we went to town we stayed in overnight and actually went to a movie. There hasn't been a single first-rate picture in over a year here, so we just decided to go anyway, and it was fun for a change; neither we nor the Brewers had been for about a year. Then we stayed at Whitings'—the people who were out here for Christmas. I wish you knew them, for they remind me in a vague way of George Price's drawings—Dotty always has too much fun doing craft work and photography and whatnot to keep house, and they all live in a four-room apartment, with little Eric, [and] the dog, which is nearly housebroken now, and a cat which is expecting kittens, and a Hopi maid—and yet somehow they are such nice people, and we have such a good time there that we hardly notice the confusion, and it is remarkable how calm and peaceful it is even with washing hanging in the living room, and everybody having to move botanical specimens, books, toys, sewing and whatnot out of the chairs before they can sit down. It is the most amazing place I have ever seen.

The Park Service is getting a bit confused—they are not having the meeting in Coolidge this year, and we have just heard that Pipe Springs has been transferred from the Southwest Monuments to Zion National Park, and Hugh is in Washington for three months. And we aren't getting any more of Budlong's wonderful reports about the mice drowning in the last of the drinking water and all the terrible hardships he used to go through, as he has been transferred to Fort Jefferson. Times are certainly changing and everyone wonders what next . . . but it is still the same old Southwest, and the spirit is still the same, at least in the outlying places. . . .

We are finding more good programs on the radio all the time and have advanced to the point that we have the news with breakfast just like everybody else. . . . We almost always have dinner music, which particularly pleases Davy. The nicest thing about a radio is the feeling that perhaps we are listening to the same things that our friends and family are listening to, and it makes us seem so close to everyone. . . .

We are all wild about a new bird book . . . —it is Roger Tory Peterson's *Field Guide to Western Birds* and you actually can find just what the bird is; it is the first one that has been simple enough for us. . . .

> *Wupatki*
> February 20, 1942

Dear Lizzie Begay,

. . . We keep wondering just what is going to happen in the Park Service, but so far things are going pretty much the same as ever. One of the monuments was transferred to Zion and they aren't hiring any new men—as some of the present ones join the ski troops or something . . . the other boys try to fill in—for instance Paul goes to Montezuma Castle [National Monument, south of Flagstaff] six days a month to relieve Earl Jackson for his days off. There won't be any meeting in Coolidge this year—to save tires and so on—and we all miss it a lot. . . .

. . . We stopped at the trading post on this side [of the Little Colorado River], run by Mary and Emmett Kellam.

They are really characters. They live in a trailer, and have this little sort of shack for the post. We all stood around in it and drank pop, and when we were leaving, Mary said, "Come and see our new cistern," and Emmett said, "Mary, you know we aren't going to have no cistern," and she said, "Oh yes we will," and took us around the corner and there was a tremendous hole with a ladder down into it and picks and shovels and buckets in it. She let us admire it awhile and then said, "Emmett started it but he got tired after a couple of hours and I have been finishing it." She is just amazing— we are wondering if she built the trading post too. She does her own washing—they haul all their water—and irons with flatirons, and runs the trading post. . . .

Wupatki
March 16, 1942

Dear Lizzy Begay,

Well, you would be surprised at Wupatki! It is almost back to where it was when we first came here except that we have the house. The CCC suddenly has been called away, and they are packing everything up and storing it and in a few days we will be alone, but entirely. It is all sudden and surprising for we all thought they would be here till summer. They have the basement of the administration building finished, but it will be just covered up until the war is over. . . . The boys from this camp will go into the Forest Camp, as that will be kept on to fight fires. Although the war is probably on our minds less than it is in more crowded parts of the country, still I think we see some of the deeper effects of it. The way we are being cut down is remarkable too—now we are to start going to town only once a month, and get the mail just once a week. . . . Davy got me a gasoline iron last month, and

am I glad now—we will be able to get our laundry sent
out twice a month, but in-between times I can do some of
it. It is quite exciting to think of, and will seem more like
a romantic Western existence, and of course we will be
able to get a lot done, not having to go to town all the
time. . . .

The Museum wants me to give a little Tuesday talk on
our bird friends—really sort of a technical topic—the
birds which are unusual in this area. So this week I spent
most of the time copying our notes off onto the observa-
tion files—imagine, we hadn't put them on the cards since
last May! I finished yesterday, and now it will be fun ar-
ranging the data. We have enough notes on the birds now
to be able to see just what we should watch for, and I think
it will be more fun observing them when we are trying to
get special information. It will be interesting to see
whether they will come into the patio when we get things
growing well. You know last year we had so many hum-
mingbirds, and we had never seen them around before. . . .

Well, it is almost time to get supper. I hope to have con-
veyed the suppressed excitement and feeling of being all
out for something or other that we have here now.

Wupatki
March 27, 1942

Dear M.—

. . . I can imagine that you often think that life in New
York is like being in another world compared with the
Southwest—but you know life here isn't glowing with joy,
fresh air and excitement all the time, and if you were in
Tucson you would probably have to do very much what
you are doing right now. . . . Flagstaff is getting ready
slowly, and really I think they have made a lot of progress

in training and planning. . . . We don't get in on it much,
just vicariously . . . stick by [the work]—it is so badly
needed. I wonder if you realize the feeling of those who
know little or nothing about the work?—That if crises
arise, there are people prepared to take initiative and to
guide and direct and prevent utter panic?

Well, maybe it is the late hour that makes me run on
like that. We were just listening to the news. Good to hear
how the English are hitting back, and we were just talking
about how really exciting the next five years or so are
going to be. The changes will be terrific in everyone's lives
and it just fills me with thrills and curiosity. I think you are
right about the different set of values we will all have. Of
course some of us have had those values all along, but no
one has had a chance to use them exclusively.

You would be amazed at Wupatki, as are we. It is just
about where it was when we came in, except that we are in
the house. All of a sudden the CCC camp went out—just
in a few days, and what an upheaval. We had just decided
to take a little vacation while it was at all possible—no relief is available, but the camp seemed surely settled till
July—so one of the foremen was going to watch the place
for us and we were all set for a couple of weeks in
Tucson—had everyone notified, and were going to have a
really ideal time—a couple of days or so with all the good
friends—when suddenly whish—and it was all off. Well,
it was fun planning and maybe we can do it some other
time—anyway now there is loads to be done here and the
life has changed so completely that it is all new and different—as good as a vacation, really. They had the basement
for the administration building ready—it is just sitting
there and Davy has to put a little roof over it. There is a
lot to be arranged and taken care of and we have new signs
to put out and the old ones to repaint. Then they stored a

lot of stuff at the camp at Heiser Spring, and we are to inspect it daily—and just as we had that news we were ra-
tioned on mileage! Which gives us a nice four-mile hike
every day. Really, M., you know how grand that is. It is
wonderful to have something to get us out every day, and
the exercise will be wonderful—it is mostly level and a
beautiful walk—we go prepared with the bird book, and
field glasses, and the lone tree at the spring is always simply loaded with birds of the most tantalizing varieties.

The rationing has other effects: we will now go to town
once a month, and for the mail every Monday only. The
trader from Black Falls has offered to pick us up some fresh
meat and lettuce and stuff between times so we will manage nicely about food, and it is a relief to not have to go to
town so often—it is really a wearing trip, and we had cut it
to once every two weeks of our own accord. This will give
us lots of extra time to do what we want to do and it looks
as if we might at last accomplish some of the things which
we had been hoping for. . . .

Now it's spring—although it still snows in town—we
have the front lawn coming up nicely and some more
bushes in, and it is the kind of weather you just want to dig
and putter outside all the time. Mrs. Colton gave me some
gorgeous asters, and they came up—then they disappeared—then they came up—they disappeared—so I
finally thought I was losing my mind. But the mystery
turned out to be our dear little wildlife gnawing them to
the ground at frequent intervals. It meant a little carpentry
for Davy, putting screen on frames to foil the mice—that
worked fine till they found they could dig under it but I
have them fixed now, I hope. I don't know how much of
that a plant will stand—did you have to contend with anything like that in Tucson? I do want something I can pick
this summer besides snakeweed and rabbit brush. . . .

Courtney and Davy on their weekly trip to the mailbox
(Photograph by Tad Nichols)

Picnic at the mailbox (Photograph by Tad Nichols)

Our "Guesties" are at low ebb and none expected in the immediate future, but the "Visities" (tourists) are coming in at the rate of a car a day, which is amazing and unexpected. Grand people too—I've been back at the guiding a bit as the Ranger is laid low with a slight cold for a couple of days and confining his activities to mystery story reading for a change. It's a good vacation for him.

Wupatki
March 29, 1942

Dear Gagoo and Aunt Clara,

. . . It seems very peaceful here, and we are starting on a full month here without going to town. Had company for supper a week ago today, and we have about one carload of visitors a day, but otherwise we don't see many people out-

side of the Navajos. . . . We are surprised to have so many
visitors coming in the fifteen miles over rough roads but
those who say anything about it say that they would have
to use their cars every day at home anyway, and so decided
that they would take a good vacation with them while they
were able. One of the custodians down south asked one of
their visitors why he was travelling now, and the man said,
"Well, we like to see things and I guess we'll just travel till
we wear out the tires and then travel on the rims."

Clyde, the Navajo, stays here while we go to town. He
came over last time, very important, with his father's bow
and arrows. Davy asked him if he was going to hunt rabbits and he said he was just practicing so he could use
them on anyone who tried to steal anything while we were
gone. . . .

Wupatki
July 1942

Dear Folksies,

. . . We did have Eric here . . . and it was just wonderful.
We certainly miss him now, and he is certainly a darling
child. They have really done a fine job of training him and
bringing him up, and although he seems spoiled at times
around his parents, he certainly was perfectly good out
here—maybe he just didn't know what he could get away
with! We had him ten days, and he was simply a model all
the time. He started out the first night after going to bed
(they told us he would sing for some time) by yelling for
water—and we thought what with it being about twice as
hot, maybe he was dying of thirst, so we got him a drink—
but the yelling kept on, and we decided it was just for
amusement, so we ignored him, and didn't have any more
trouble. Incidentally, he sings Gilbert and Sullivan. It was

Charley Clyde Peshlakai (Photograph by John L. Blackford)

terrifically hot compared to Flag, so we had to accustom
him to the sun gradually. He is crazy about the little lizards
that live in the patio walls, so we could take him out several times a day to look at them. After we got his schedule
fixed in our minds, life was very simple, although I don't
know how mothers have time to do much beside being
mothers. . . .

One night we had to go to see Clyde, who was at the
river, planting, and we got Eric up after he had been in bed
about half an hour, and took him along. We surely were
glad we did, for he and Charley Clyde just had a whirl.
They just chattered away in their respective languages, and
Sally had a fine time teaching Navajo words to Eric who
would repeat anything she would say—he could learn the

language in about a week I think, since he talks incessantly.
They had a little kitten, a baby rabbit, a tame little goat,
and the two little boys just whooped around with the pets.
Catherine has a new little baby girl now too. It is the tin-
iest baby I have ever seen, and I think quite premature, but
apparently thriving. . . .

Wupatki
July 4, 1942

Dear M.,
. . . We miss you a lot, and wish we could see you. We
are going to try to get at the furniture building again, and
there is lots to be done. How are you at painting signs?
Can you run a posthole auger? That is my latest accom-
plishment. If you think any of these jobs sound enticing
you may take us up on them.

As to leaving, it does not seem so near as we were thinking. But we don't know why it should not come—after all,
if there is gas rationing out here no one could get to
Wupatki, and it occasionally irks Davy to feel that he is
not doing as much as he can for the country. He is plenty
busy, and it is all necessary work in one sense, but in another sense he thinks everyone should pitch right in and
get the war over with, and not fool around about it. They
may give us a shortwave radio, and then he will feel somewhat differently as he could be of more assistance by
checking up on what goes on out here and reporting
things. Some fairly important connective roads go through
here, and we keep close watch on all the travel.

We don't get much Park Service news anymore since
there just aren't any technicians going around inspecting
and carrying rumors anymore. Do you remember that the
girls [HCWPs—"Honorary Custodians Without Pay"—the

wives of the custodians, who did the same work as their husbands without pay or official recognition] of the Southwest Monuments started a little round robin sort of paper after the Boss died [two years earlier] so we could keep in touch with what was going on everywhere? Well, it . . . had finally given out—but Sallie Brewer and I got worried about it enough to bring it back and are working like beavers editing and publishing. We had to type [all the copies of] the first issue by hand—a ghastly job, but we have someone to mimeograph it now, and it should go pretty well. It is a month-and-a-halfly if there is such a thing, entitled *THE GRAPEVINE.* We hope it helps, the second issue is almost due, and soon we will know how it goes. . . .

Wupatki
July 14, 1942

Dear Lizzie Begay,
    . . . We went to town for the Hopi Craftsman, and of course it was a bit dumb trying to get our supplies on the Fourth of July, in the midst of the Pow-Wow Parade, but aside from that it was a delightful trip. . . . The Craftsman was just beautiful, and for once I got to watch all the people at work, weaving, making baskets, and pottery, as much as I wanted to, for I worked out there all afternoon and evening. All the things on display are entered for prizes of course, and are the finest things made on the reservation all year, but they are also for sale, at the prices the Hopi put on them, and we had to handle that, get the money and give people their receipts, and so on. I learned a lot about the Hopi, and really sold loads of stuff. . . .
    The next most exciting thing around here was the fire. This has been such a dry year that they are just going crazy worrying about fires, what with no CCC boys to

help anymore, and have had training schools for all the high school boys. Well, one afternoon the haze, which is usually dust, got thicker all of a sudden and what should it be but smoke, just rolling over the edge of the mesa above the house and pouring down toward the river. It was very strong too. Davy and Clyde and Andy, another Navajo who was one of the CCC boys at the Navajo CCC camp across the river, and who married the medicine man's cute daughter, were cleaning the spring, and as it was about quitting time, Davy asked if they would go to the fire with him. He climbed the Mesa and the fire was over north of the Peaks (it looked and smelled like it was right on top of us). Clyde wasn't very anxious to go, as he had fought a forest fire before, but Andy said he would so both of them did.

Andy's wife and little boy were camped down here, and she came up to stay with me all night. Her name is Helen, and she doesn't speak a word of English. But she is a very sweet girl and very neat and fastidious. Davy thought she might sleep in the patio, but there are owls around here, and they think they are ghosts, so I told her she could sleep in the living room. We couldn't converse, really, but if we made up our minds what we were going to do we could tell each other all right. . . . [I climbed the mesa but] I couldn't see the fire for the smoke, but the sunset was gorgeous, and I came down and we sat out here by the house and looked through the [field] glasses . . . and then came in and had devil's food cake with boiled icing, which was the first good chocolate cake I have ever made. Then we went to bed, she sleeping on the davenport. In the morning . . . while I was wondering if she would be here for breakfast she gathered up Kimmy and said they were going home. . . .

Davy got home at about noon, covered with smoke and

soot. They had worked fourteen-and-a-half hours continuously and without eating. After he ate, the dope went out and I found him guiding visities so sent him home. He was quite O.K. the next day. And was he glad he had come home—they thought the fire was under control but it got going and they had to bring men in from Kingman, Ashfork, Prescott, Williams, etc. and it took two more days to put it out! They are going to have Davy watch for fires down our way and bring Navajos. Clyde & Andy made $9.40 each—alas! Davy can't draw pay for it!

Guess what we are in town for—a water tank and a heavier truck! The spring got so low Davy & Clyde cleaned it, but it is just putting out a trickle. We haven't been able to water the lawn for two weeks and are practically out of water. So we are going to haul from Heiser. Every time we flush the john we worry! So Davy will get a big tank and we'll be O.K. . . .

Wupatki
July 30, 1942

Dear Folksies,

. . . The Park Service is still quite intact—some of the boys have gone to the Army, but they are spreading the others around in their places. Our Superintendent, who was just wonderful, has become the head of all the Park Service personnel, in charge of appointments and such in Washington, and the Assistant Superintendent is now Superintendent. He is quite a different type of fellow from anyone we have had before but the change will be a good thing in times like this, we think.

We went up to Sunset Crater last Monday, to spend the day putting up signs and cleaning up the paper plates and junk. When we got there it began to rain and kept it up intermittently all the time. Davy would dig a hole and put in a sign and we would run like mad for the car and wait till it let up a little, then he would finish that sign and start another, and we would run for the car again. There was one terrible clap of thunder, and we thought it might have hit something, but we couldn't see anything; then, just as we were leaving to come home, we saw smoke coming from where we had heard the noise. So it was probably a forest fire, right there on the monument, and we had to go. I had never seen one up close, and was very excited.

We drove as far as we could, then took the shovel and axe and a crowbar and a big thermos of water and started on foot. About a mile away was the fire, and it was just one big dead tree, with the bottom, up to about seven feet high, burning. The lightning had blown off one side of it and all the branches, and there was lots of dry stuff and pine needles around the bottom. Davy began chopping off the burning stuff with the axe and I would shovel it up and carry it to a bare place and scatter it so the rain could put it out. It was just getting into the pitch. We couldn't have stopped it if that had really started to burn, but we got it all out in about an hour and a half. We had to dig out some of the roots and put them out too. It was very interesting, but I was glad it wasn't a bad fire. Then we saw another one up on the Peaks where the lookout can't see, so we went to a farm and called and reported it, and finally we got to go home. It was very beautiful coming home, as the sun would break through once in a while and hit some of the far mesas, and they would just glow with bright red and orange in the midst of all the blue shadows. . . .

Yesterday we had .96 of an inch of rain in twenty-five minutes. It was wonderful to watch, but by the time it quit it was raining harder in the house than it was outside. They have never gotten this roof fixed right, and it leaked in our

closet, the living room, kitchen, dining room, on the book-
case in Davy's office and so on, till we were just tearing
around lickety-cut with pans and bath towels. We would
find them all and suddenly there would come an awful
sound of rushing water and there it would be pouring in
someplace else. Davy had just gone all over the roof with
tar and gravel, too, but I guess it just has to be re-roofed. . . .

Wupatki
September 21, 1942

Dear M.,
    . . . Somehow we thought you might be out for October
—but with nationwide gas rationing I suppose it's out—
anyway the gas rationing all over makes us feel better out
here. It is beautiful, though—I just have to tell you. This
morning there was that wide band of orange around the
middle of the Peaks which means the aspens are turning,
and all the way to the mailbox the road was simply lined
with fields of purple asters, the best we have ever seen, and
clumps of orange and yellow flowers—and all day and
night the heavy sweet fragrance of the golden buckwheat
on the mesa drifts down through our windows. . . .
    This is the week we will make the monthly trip to town,
which is doubly exciting this time. For one, Davy is going
to talk to an Army Air Corps recruiting officer—we hear
they are anxious to get archaeologists (the only people
who seem to want them) for Plotting Officers! But really,
from what we have read, his geology and photography
training and experience are just exactly what they list and
it seems just the place. We're really excited about it, and
although our new Superintendent tells us that it is really
patriotic to stay here until drafted, Davy just doesn't feel
right about it. I've been job scouting a bit—could get lots

Nez ka Yazzie, the medicine man, and a sandpainting at Hal Smith's hogan, 1939 (Photograph by Tad Nichols)

of different things here in Flag—but would like outdoor work if possible—they think the Park Service may put in more girl rangers, and I hope I can qualify. Of course I'll go with Davy as long as I can, but don't want to just sit around. Will keep you posted. . . .

. . . We have tons of news all the time [for the *Grapevine*] and got permission from Miss Story to put in official news, and it is rather booming along with six pages per copy. . . . Everybody says it helps morale, which is just exactly what we did it for so we feel rewarded! I hadn't seen her [Sallie Brewer] since May. . . . In the afternoon we went to a Sing. Clyde was having one for a sore knee, looked like an infection to us, and we were talking hospital to him, but he had a three-day Sing and is O.K. That was the first day, when

Sal and I went, and then Davy and I saw the other two
sandpaintings.[28] They were wonderful too—the most elab-
orate and lovely we have ever seen. Such lovely colors,
rust, blue, yellow, and black and white, on a beige sand
background. Anyway, the medicine man said the trouble
with the knee was this: Two years ago, Clyde rode a horse
which had been struck by lightning. The lightning put
some evil spirits into the horse, and while Clyde was riding
along on it, his knee rubbed against it, till some of the evil
came out of the horse and went into his knee. So they had
special lightning sandpaintings, and Clyde would sit on
them and they would sing. That would make some good
spirits come out of the sandpainting and go into him and
push out the evil. As I said before he is all right now, and
so he won't have to go to the hospital where they would
probably cut off his leg, because they don't know any way
to get that evil out.

Sally and Catherine's sister, the educated one, Modesta,
came over with her husband, Bill Dixon, and their five children. They came in a coupe which they had borrowed for
twenty-five dollars—and did they get their money's worth.
Of course the Peshlakai family was just delighted, and the
car was a wreck, so Bill would work on it for about four
hours, and then they would all get in and take the medicine man up to the mountains for more medicine, and then
Bill would work awhile, and they would all get in again and
go to the farm for some corn, and Bill would clean the
spark plugs and they would go to the trading post. The last
day when Bill had to get home and get the kids in school,
some relatives got him to take them to Tuba [City], so
they had to start home Sunday night to drive to Gallup to
get the kids in school!

We walked over several times during the festivities, and
had a fine time. Clyde was dramatic in a purple rayon

velvet shirt and a headband, and just moaning and groaning and everybody running around waiting on him. Today they all went to a Squaw Dance over at Denebito, except one boy to herd sheep, and Donald [Clyde's son], who turned out to be a peach of a kid, and he is working for Davy. He studied agriculture in school last year, and is just crazy to be a gardener. So we are encouraging him all we can. He is going to help us landscape the bare and blowing cinders around the house this fall, and will always be a big help around here, unless he gets a job somewhere. We are going to recommend him to the Coltons. He is the one we used to think was pretty no-account, but it turned out to be bad company, I guess, or just a phase. . . .

Would you believe we had a cat? . . . The mice were eating their way through the walls, to say nothing of the fifth planting of lettuce, and the trading post had a "nice young mouser" who has become our little pet kitty. We are quite silly about her but are giving her away this week. . . . Yesterday I caught her chasing a bird, and although it got away under its own power, she had a bunch of feathers in her mouth—so goodbye kitty. I suppose it is foolish to try to discriminate between birds and rodents! . . .

Wupatki
October 22, 1942

Dear Moth and Ganga,

. . . I certainly had a nice offer the other day—Mrs. Colton wrote that although they knew I would want to be with Davy if possible, if I couldn't go along wherever he went, they would like me to come in and work for Dr. Colton as stenographer and assistant, and part of the pay would be to live with them. . . . I imagine if it came to getting a job, that is the one I would take. I hadn't realized how worried Davy was about what I would do. He was certainly touched by that offer, and said he would rather know that I was with someone I liked than anything, and was only worried about whether I would be happy up there, and whether that country or anything would depress me—wasn't that nice? Of course it would be depressing to live in Flag, but it is quite different out at the Museum, and the work would be very interesting. . . .

Wupatki
December 2, 1942

Dear M.,

As you see, we are still here at Wupatki, but for how long we just don't know. Davy has been actively trying to enlist but it seems as if there is a slight hitch to nearly everything for which he is qualified. Leads about new places to try are still being followed, though, and if he finds something in which he can be useful, and where he may get experience which will be helpful later, he will sign up in January or February; otherwise he will stick to Wupatki until the draft board gets around to him. I have some good chances for jobs, so he is relieved of worry about me and is free to go ahead. . . .

One Monday we had word that Mother, Father, and Aunt Maude were going to drive out, and hoped to be here on the next Wednesday. As we were in town, there was much bustle but I was glad not to have time to clean house or anything. They arrived on Davy's birthday by driving pretty long hours, and oh what cheers and whoops of joy. Mother had never seen Wupatki, and of course I had about given up hopes of getting them all out here before we had to depart. As it happened, they only had three days here, since Dad had to get back to work, but the visit couldn't have been more perfect, weather and all. They were just rare—we were sleeping in the trailer so as not to disturb them in the morning, and when we came tiptoeing in, there they were all lined up in chairs in front of the living room windows watching the beginnings of the sunrise, with appropriate squeals and yelps as it advanced. We didn't go far afield, but took in things like Wukoki and the river and Clyde's family, where they got to see Sally string up a rug from the very beginning.

We had Thanksgiving in at Coltons' [after the family's departure] with a great feeling of thankfulness for a return to a more simple and useful kind of living—most appropriately, we had milk and butter from their own cow, and other home-grown things, which made it seem like an old-fashioned ceremony. Then they came out for a last look at some of the ruins before gas rationing set in—stayed Saturday and Sunday nights, and we had some fine long hikes, and got to see a lot of the monument which was new to us. . . .

We're bustling around trying to get the monument all fixed up, besides painting furniture, making Christmas cards . . . and a lot of other little projects. . . . Never get so eager to furnish a house that you put in the furniture before it is finished! It is certainly hard to take it out again when you are accustomed to using it.

I went around to the recruiting office to see about the WAACs when we were in town. Sallie Brewer had been so excited about them and had talked to a lady lieutenant, and found out a lot. . . . A girl Davy's age and height would have to weigh more than ten pounds more than he does—isn't it amazing? We wondered if they were going to use the WAACs for military police—they seemed to want really hefty gals. I guess you didn't know that Jimmy Brewer enlisted in the Sea Bees, and will be called any day now, so Sallie is really making some investigations. You

know she has the same rating as Jean [McWhirt], and
might go into the Park Service, although they are really
looking more for clerks than rangers.

Did you know Headquarters moved to Santa Fe? There
was a nice big building so that seemed the obvious thing to
do—but they are farther from us now, not that it makes
much difference—we just don't pop into the truck and
dash off to Headquarters [at Coolidge] anymore! . . .

Wupatki
January 2, 1943

Dear M.,

How wonderful to have the *New Yorker* and *Atlantic*
again—M., you are surely grand to send them, for there is
nothing which could possibly give us more pleasure, and
they make all the difference in our morale, and keep us
feeling really civilized. . . . We are able to talk intelligently
and keep a good perspective on what is going on in the
world outside Wupatki.

We thought of you so much at Christmas, realizing how
different it must be for you, and hoping that you did have
a nice day. We didn't get to go to Gallup, but we went
down to Gray Mountain Trading Post Christmas Eve and
spent the next two days with the Reids and Stanfills there.
They are grand folks and make us feel so at home. Christmas Eve we had an assembly line and filled sacks of fruit
and candy for the nearby Navajos, which was almost as
much fun as seeing them get them in the morning. And
everyone surely loves the Reids, so that all the time people
were dropping in to wish them Merry Christmas—people
from highway camps, ranches, and other trading posts—
and of course the drinks went round every time someone
came in, so it was most gay. We got to see all the "neigh-

bors" clear up to The Gap, and then there were fourteen
for dinner, and we had one of their own homegrown tur-
keys. We played poker in the evening, and then the next
day Mrs. Moore from Spider Web Ranch came back and
taught us a new rummy game which we played nearly all
day.

Gallup, New Mexico
January 12, 1943

Dear Liz,

We came over to Davy's folks' on Sunday, so I'm writing
at odd moments. . . . Sallie and Jim Brewer have gone to
her folks—he should be called any day. She has applied for
[a] Park Service job and may get one, as she had a ranger
exam and passed. She was also thinking of the WAACs—
they say anyone with a college education has a good
chance of getting officer's training, and she thought she'd
take radio operating. . . . Katharine Bartlett . . . is teaching
Red Cross first aid and taking a Motor Division course in
the care of cars, which must be wonderful. She says everyone should be required to have it when they get a license.

I'm putting out the *Grapevine* alone this month. . . .

Wupatki
February 6, 1943

Dear Folksies,

. . . At Davy's folks we spent several days just doing
things around the place. . . . Davy made a washstand and
cupboard, and we cleaned up the storeroom, which is quite
a task as Davy's mother wants to keep everything. She even
has Mary's wedding cake, and costumes the kids used in
grade school, which is about like our family, of course. The

most interesting thing was that she was worried about mice
getting into the old Germantown yarn Navajo rugs they
have, so Davy got all the histories on them and we
brought them home and will put them in storage with our
stuff. They are simply stunning—bright red backgrounds,
and Davy says they are the best he has ever seen. . . . I
love to get Davy's mother talking about the early days in
that country. She came out to take nurse's training in Albuquerque when she was about 17, and it was still a wild and
woolly country. She has tons of lovely presents from people in mining towns and so on, that is how they have some
of those lovely rugs. . . .

In Albuquerque . . . [we] call[ed] on friends . . . and
Davy went all around looking for jobs in the Army, Navy
and so on, and I looked for jobs at the Soil Conservation
Service and Forest Service, which would both take me on
as a draftsman, which gave me a lot of confidence. . . . The
SCS was perfectly keen, nice people and very helpful, but
that would be a last resort for me. Drafting is terribly over-
crowded in peacetime, and I would rather learn something
which would be useful after the war. . . . I put in the letter
to Dad about getting word from Dr. Colton that I could
have the Museum job whenever I wanted it, so of course
that is what I will do, but at the time we were in Albuquerque it seemed very uncertain and I thought I simply must
find out if there was anything else I could do. Only *no one* is
supposed to know about what I am going to do, you know.

Well, Santa Fe was wonderful. The day we got there,
there was snow packed in the streets up to the curbs, and
the next afternoon when we left the streets were running
bank-full of water. That is such a rare town. The down-
town part is of course over 300 years old, older of course
than any town in the East, and the roads are just trails; I
guess there is hardly a two-way street in the place. . . . We

went out to the Park Service building that afternoon and you never saw anything like it. It is huge and all full of patios, and the main offices have fireplaces, and Navajo rugs, and the conference room has carved furniture, and there is a Coke machine outside the naturalists' office and the naturalists, Natt [Dodge] and Eric Reid, have a fund for the entertainment of visitors. Actually they are quite cut down on stenographers and such but it still looks like acres of them. That night Natt and Hap had everyone come over and showed movies of the various monuments, and we got to see all our friends, and we surely had a fine time. We also saw the superintendent's house in the afternoon and it is the acme of what you expect in Santa Fe—big cool-looking whitewashed rooms, and their hand-carved furniture and lovely rugs look very stunning. . . .

Davy is doing something interesting now—every two weeks he writes a letter, with carbon copies, for the Navajo boys from around here who are in the Army. They get so homesick, and of course, their folks can't write. . . . The part that takes time is that the families come up every few days and give us news to put in the letter. They sit around for about two hours before they say what they came for, so it is sometimes hard to be patient and wait for it. . . .

I guess I didn't tell you that the Navajos have named Catherine's little girl "Eleanor" for the President's wife!

Wupatki
March 3, 1943

Dear M.,

. . . We had a wire from Mr. Buchenberg, the man who lived in the trailer and did so much work here, that he had loaned his very fine shortwave radio to the Navy and could we please get it disconnected and send it off for him in a hurry. So we dashed into town with it last Saturday. While we were in town, Davy went in to talk to the draft board again. They had said they would call him about the first of April, but he found them still a bit uncertain of when he would be needed. Consequently he volunteered for enlistment. They think he will go to Phoenix for the examinations about the fifth of April. I'm glad he decided to take things in his own hands, for the uncertainty was hard on him, and besides there is a better chance of his getting into the work he would like by volunteering. When he leaves, I am going to try to get back to Nebraska before settling down to a job. After all, it is over three years since we went back there, and I can hardly stand the fact that there [are] two darling little nieces since the last visit. I'm quite sure that I'll be in Flagstaff for the duration. . . .

Things happen so fast around here. Did I tell you that we have a radio telephone? We talk to Paul at Walnut Canyon every evening at 5:30. We are KNKF, and he is KNKE. We have a whole new vocabulary. The Navajos are so disappointed that the radio doesn't talk Navajo—but perhaps the trader down at the river is going to arrange to get the Window Rock news broadcasts for them. Clyde was working here one day and got to hear the broadcast, and the next day Sally, Catherine, and the two children arrived at 1:30 and settled down to wait!

We are going to plant a vegetable garden in the back patio this week—will haul in some good dirt when we go out for the mail and then will have to build some screened frames to keep the mice and rats away. We still don't know who will be here but they will need some greenery to help eke out the [food] coupons. Maybe it is a good thing Davy is going to the Army where he will get something to eat— all we can get each month is two cans of tomatoes! I did rig up a fine place to keep fresh fruit and vegetables in

Sally (*center*) and Catherine Peshlakai fixing the hair of their niece
Louise Chee, daughter of Ruby and Julius Chee (Photograph by
Tad Nichols)

quantity—it is made of the screened trays of a sherd-
drying rack. Archaeology is such a practical profession! . . .

We've been having lots of company. . . . Yesterday we
took some friends down to the river, and there in the middle, with the water running full force, was a Navajo wagon.
It had been abandoned to the elements in midstream the
night before—all aboard having been able to unload the
wagon and finish the trip on foot. Mary Kellam, the trader's
wife, looked at it with much concern, since there is still a
twenty-five dollar payment due on it.

Wupatki
March 15, 1943

Dear Liz the Whiz,

Oh, boy! Do you really think we can be home together? Wouldn't it be fun? Well, all I know now is that Davy volunteered for enlistment—will take blood test in town March 24—then to Phoenix for exams on about April 5th. One week off, during which we will go to Gallup. Since we will be that far on the way, I'll probably leave from there and will have until May 1st to get back to Flag. That means I'll be home the last half of April, providing all goes according to schedule. I'll let you know. . . .

Lots of news but no time to write—Sallie Brewer is *Ranger* at Casa Grande [Ruins National Monument]—lives at Vahki Inn. No uniform yet—she's the first permanent girl ranger we know of. Supt. said he would do some research and not let her be outdone by the WAACs! . . .

Box 601, Flagstaff
June 6, 1943

Dear M.,

. . . Don't worry about the noncommittal address—it conceals the possible alternative of "Coyote Range," which I thought a little fancy. That is the name of Coltons' place—and I am staying with them! Isn't that something? But really that was the deciding factor, for it meant a nice homelife with such likeable and pleasant people, and good food (cow & chickens & gardens), and I have a room with fireplace. Latter runs all the time I am sitting in there as it is darn cold here—really freezing the last couple of nights, but very lovely and crisp in the daytime and many flowers in bloom.

Sallie Brewer at Casa Grande Ruins National Monument,
circa 1943–44 (Photographer unknown, courtesy of Courtney
Reeder Jones)

You and the cooking—you used to be simply wonderful
at it. . . . It really is tough to plan meals now that you are
cut down to just a dab of meat now and then—at least we
are, having two ravenous dogs without ration cards. I am
doing the meal planning and marketing; the cooking is
done by Pauline, a sweet little Navajo girl, who has the
most charming and original hairdos, and the most gentle
disposition and sweet personality of any I have ever run

across. Her husband is in the Marines—in the special Navajo battalion at first and now in the South Pacific. He is about to get a commission.

You bet we are in the forest. Did you see Coltons' house when you were up to the AAAS meeting? It has lovely views straight out to the Peaks, and is surrounded by pines. Katharine Bartlett lives here too, and she and I water the grass and various things like that outside after work. . . . We both work here in the lab in the mornings, then walk about a mile to the Museum in the afternoon, and it is a charming walk, on a little path through ravines and across meadows and through the woods.

I finally got an Arizona driver's license—at last, you must say. So I can drive down for groceries, three miles to town. I go in once a week, taking Mrs. McKee (her husband is Assistant Director—he taught in Tucson (geology) this winter), and then once [a week I ride] with her. Katharine and I have saved enough gas to see some of the sights. I had never seen the ski area. The trip up reminds me of the time you took me up to Mount Lemmon, and you can see all over from there. Also got up on Observatory Mesa, where the Lowell Observatory is. I had never been, and it is only about half a mile from town!

We went out to read the rain gauges last week—they are read once every three months—and there are some out near Wupatki, so we went in there. It did seem most strange and weird to have someone else living in the house, but somehow I didn't mind. It was one of those DAYS. The wind was blowing like a good old Arizona spring, and you couldn't see the desert, and the dust was coming through the steel windows and drifting in the bathtub, and I just thought I was well out of it for awhile. Of course I would have felt differently in October, for instance, or if there were no war, but I have my mind made up that this is my life for the time being, so don't seem to miss Wupatki. The boys out there are taking good care of things [and] have a bull snake in the front patio to eat the rats and mice. Purely a matter of preference—snakes or cats, take your pick; you have to have one or the other, if you are going to raise shrubs and flowers. Katharine and I peeled sweaters all the way down, and put them on in layers on the way back up.

Davy is making a fine adjustment, I think. He really is trying to get everything he can out of all the new experiences, and in many ways I know we both will benefit. We would not exactly choose to have things turn out like this, although he did volunteer; but just the same a little shake-up changes the point of view and outlook, and I know we will go on with many new and refreshing ideas. . . .

Flagstaff
September 5, 1943

Dear M.,

. . . Davy was moved to Denver, to Lowry Field, with a promotion to PFC ($4 a month more!), and is so happy to be in the West. . . . I went up to see him when he got there, and am about to go up again as he will be through the 25th of this month, and we have no idea where he will go, although we have hopes of the next stop being Colorado Springs. He got just exactly what he wanted, and I guess I shouldn't be surprised, but you do hear of misfits and dismal situations. He is taking phototopography, which is making maps of aerial photos and interpreting the pictures. He's been doing just splendidly in it, and has been spending every evening studying except to go out on his day off. He has passed the physical for overseas duty, and will go in January, unless he is picked for an instructor, which I am sure will disappoint him—but it wouldn't disappoint me a bit. . . .

Tuesday

Just got back from seminar—[the] talk was about "The personality of Pachygrapsus, a common shore crab," and given by one of the little Navy boys at the college here for a bit more education. They have a whole bunch of these boys going to school here—two come out here often, and they have been taking trips on the weekends and collecting scorpions for me. I gave a talk on scorpions a few weeks ago—had a lovely big Wupatki specimen—alive— and told them all I could manage to find out, especially about the deadly ones. Am having all the museum specimens identified, and am about to collect some black widow spiders too, and maybe get up a little exhibit of these little animals. . . .

Oklahoma City
February 22, 1944

Dear M.,

. . . As the Coltons have held my job for me, I shall return to Flag when Davy leaves and probably work there all summer. . . . Everyone seems to have so many problems now. They say the Americans are fighting this war so they can come home, and I suppose it is true of every country. They all just want to get it over and get back, and I do hope that when they get back they will really appreciate and enjoy what they have. Maybe we needed shaking up. I'm idealistic enough to feel that they are really coming back to a better world. . . .

Flagstaff
May 2, 1944

Dear M.,

. . . Davy . . . has landed in England, and I am getting mail fairly regularly now. Some of it a month old, and some a week old, but it comes anyway. . . . He has such great interest in people and places that I think that he will get a great deal out of being in England and find friends and pleasure there. He described in great and wonderful detail the countryside—the farms, with hedgerows, and cottages with thatched roofs (cut off neatly like the Hopis cut their hair) and some trees on the horizon which looked like hills. Later he wrote that the fog cleared away, and darned if they weren't hills! . . .

I came right back here from Oklahoma City, thinking it was best to get right to work—and boy, do I work. No help, so I get noon dinner for the family three days a week, and Katie and I get supper every night. Sometimes it seems like a long old day to come home from work and keep at it till eight, but I kick myself now and then and think, well, it keeps me busy, anyway. I love my work dearly. Perhaps it is not the best thing to live with the Coltons besides working here, but we all get along splendidly and I am much happier than I ever thought I would be. Had considered going to be with the folks, but think that this is the best place for me. . . .

Dr. [Colton] is working on a book on all the archaeology that has been done here in the last 25 years, so I got to go through all the files and am now doing drawings for publication. Golly—to read about the dear wild Tsegi country—it surely inflames the old wanderlust. And now I am putting up an exhibition of kachina dolls—what they are, the kachina calendar, and the bean dance, with labels to tell what each one does—and two little cases, one of which compares one of the kachinas with Santa Claus. You know I am kind of proud of it and am doing it mostly myself, although Dr. is helping a lot and today Mrs. Colton came over for an hour and assisted. . . .

Sallie Brewer is about to transfer to Tumacacori [National Monument, near Nogales]. She says there could be no finer boss than Al Bicknell, but that she simply can't stand another summer of weather over 110 degrees. . . . And Paul Beaubien of Walnut is being torn away for the duration to go to Saguaro. . . .

Flagstaff
May 26, 1944

Dear Marian,

. . . The kachina exhibit has been a great success—did I tell you we dressed a window dummy up like a full-sized one, with a mask and costume? I got hysterical while I was trying to dress it. . . . Dr. and Jimmy Kay came running in and they laughed too. [Dr. Colton] is so dignified looking that it tickled me to see him laugh so hard at me and the dummy. He wears a little white goatee and mustache. He really has a wonderful sense of humor and sometimes he and I get hysterical at the table and laugh till we cry. It is just like being around you and Liz at times. . . .

The storerooms at the Museum are real cold, colder than outside, and we were mentioning it one day and Dr. said that he was taking some people through them one day and he got practically numb, and when he got to the cases of animal skins he wanted to get out the big antelope skin and wrap it around him—well, I just about had to leave the table, because I could just imagine what the people would have thought of this little dignified man with the goatee if he had calmly wrapped himself up in a skin from

one of the cases—and the more I thought about it the
more I would just nearly die laughing. . . .

Flagstaff

August 13, 1944

Dear M.,

. . . Paul [Beaubien] is definitely at Saguaro, and it is a
mess, too—they are building trail all over the mountains.
The first week he was there he was out with the string of
five pack mules, and one jumped over a cliff, taking all the
rest to their deaths—what a beginning, and I think he is
confident that the monument is eternally doomed to bad
luck. Hope not—at least it should run out before long. . . .

I do hope that fate and circumstances will bring us together again before long—you are good for my morale,
and I often think of how Davy and I used to daydream
about trying to get you to come up and fix up a ranch in
the juniper grassland near Wupatki and come over and sit
by our fire and talk to us. I hope we have enough sense not
to go back to Wupatki—that should also be a closed book,
and I'm afraid it even lasted a little too long, although I do
not believe there is any place in the world more beautiful.
Still it is the congeniality and the friends and the work
which count, and if you don't have harmony in those, the
beauty of a place doesn't count. It is exciting to not know
what the future might be like—I never mention to Davy,
nor he to me, that we might not go back, since it gives us
something definite to remember and count on, but I think
both of us feel that we have outgrown it. I don't think either of us could stand to have a paved highway running
through it! Our attitude toward the Park Service is based
entirely on the Boss's ideals, and I hope it will always be
that way. . . .

Flagstaff
October 22, 1944

Dear Family,

. . . I went to one of the men on the ration board to see
if I could get gas to go to Wupatki. Phil [van Cleave] had
been telling me to come out as he had to make a list of the
books which belonged to the monument, and he said I
should help sort out ours. Well I had no idea we had left
many and figured it didn't amount to much. . . . It was
gorgeous clear weather, and I was afraid I'd best go quickly,
and being Saturday or Sunday I wouldn't have to take a day
off; so they told me to go Sunday and they would let me
have the gas later. Boy, was I glad, and it was the most wonderful trip you could imagine. We started rather late in the
afternoon, which made such beautiful light and shadows
and the desert was perfectly clear and absolutely at its best.

It had been over a year since I had been there, and I was
so afraid I would be disappointed, but it was perfect in
every way—we even got to see all the Navajos, as they
were planning a Sing the next night—sure sorry it wasn't
that night, but we saw all of them anyway. It was to be a
Sing for Modesta's baby which has been in a hospital for
three months. Believe it or not, they had gone to borrow
the baby from the hospital for the Sing—to be returned
afterwards, of course. When we were there I would have
thought that perfectly natural, but now I can see how rare
it is, and really hope it didn't kill the baby.

When we got out there the sun was just setting, my favorite time of day, and we had taken fried chicken and so
we got the books sorted—turned out to be at least sixty!—
and then visited the Navajos, ate, and went down to see
Emmett and Mary [Kellam]. . . . I am so glad there was an
excuse to get gas to go, for it couldn't have been nicer in
any way. . . .

Davy is fine. . . . I had a lovely letter from Jean McWhirt Pinkley—she is working at Mesa Verde as naturalist again, and Addison is definitely lost. Her attitude is just wonderful and it certainly was inspiring. . . . I wish he hadn't been so set on submarine duty, but maybe it's just something that was bound to happen, and she is taking it wonderfully well. . . .

Flagstaff
July 21, 1945

Dear M.,
. . . Davy is now in—of all places—Chandler! At Williams Field. Of course they do not promise not to send him to the South Pacific, but he got this assignment due to some sinus trouble, and will be on "permanent party" as soon as he finishes two months of training. The work is much the same as he did in France. He is spending his time off looking for a place for us to live—in Chandler, Mesa, and Tempe—something is supposed to materialize by August, and meanwhile I am working here at the Museum and helping Mrs. Colton in the house, and wondering how I am going to pack and store the accumulation of stuff. . . .

Mesa
August 17, 1945

Dear Folksies,
Well, it just seems unbelievable that *the war is over*—I guess everyone feels kind of dumbfounded. . . . Davy went out to work yesterday and they sent him home. . . . On Tuesday he was home before the announcement was made—we were over at the Poisonous Animals Lab looking at the scorps! . . . We invited our landladies and the

couple who had moved into the other room to eat with us.
We couldn't go out in the evening as they announced that
all the boys would be picked up if they appeared on the
streets, so we missed all the rough stuff. The next day we
went to Phoenix, and it was covered with confetti and torn
paper and everything was closed, although we were able to
eat in one of the hotels. . . .

Davy has written . . . to see if the Park Service will ask
for a discharge for their men. If they will do that we would
go back to Wupatki and wait for a transfer. . . .

Mesa
August 26, 1945

Dear Folksies,

We are leaving in the morning for the Grand Canyon!
Davy has been assigned there as Director of Recreation at
the Army Rest Camp. We are absolutely dumbfounded, but
are just thrilled, too. . . . Davy came home excited, as he
had heard that personnel were needed at Grand Canyon
Rest Camp. He called the Park Superintendent, Dr. Bryant,
who is an old friend. Dr. B. said he'd try to help, as the
Army was clashing with the Park, and he figured Davy was
just the answer. Davy went back to the field, asked for the
job and they fell on his neck, as they'd given up hope of
getting anyone. He was listed as "essential" so it took another day to cut the red tape—but he is now signed up. . . .

Grand Canyon
November 7, 1945

Dear Liz,

. . . I also finished my paper on spinning which is to be
published by the Museum—still have to draw the illustra-

tions, but can do that while we are in Flag.[29] And they have sent me the "dummy" for my book on Navajo rugs— don't know how I can ever write it, but the dummy is simply beautiful and most inspiring. It has colored sketches and is going to have several pages of pictures. That is how publishers hook you and force you to write for them! . . .

Los Gatos, California
November 20, 1945

Dear M.,

. . . Davy is a civilian again—and looks FREE—it does make a difference . . . he was nervous as a cat and paced the floor but is settling down. We came out here to see the folks a few days ago, after three days in Flag to put more in storage, pack, etc. . . .

The Canyon interlude was swell—Davy had such good luck in the Army—but funny—you should hear of it sometime. Davy ran the camp and I bossed the cooking the last month—did it myself a couple of weeks—but it was inactive—anyway, there were lots of good NPS friends and we had a lovely time and a darling house. . . . We went over to the North Rim and got to ride the Park mule and horse clear back through the Canyon, alone, no guides—it was *wonderful*.

We probably go to Flag in about two weeks, then to Santa Fe and Albuquerque, and possibly will go out and stay at Wupatki a month or so before Davy has to go to work. He'd like to write up his "dig"—and doesn't legally have to work for the Government until February. . . .

And thanks for *Natural History*. We love it, and it's especially nice to have the magazines as we return to our more isolated existence. Davy is applying for a transfer, but we don't know where to go. He wants an administrative job. . . .

Flagstaff
December 20, 1945

Dear M.,

Thanks so much for your good letter, and the admirable suggestion for your Christmas gift, which is exactly the sort of present we like to give. It will not be a real Christmas for a long time to many people all over the world, but the possibility of real peace and happiness seems nearer when we have a letter like yours. I hope that others who have been as fortunate as we may feel the same desire to help those to whom the end of the war brings only continued misery. I can't express it as I'd like, but thank you for the suggestion and opportunity to do a little more. It is very like you, M. . . .

We intend to go to Wupatki on January first, if the papers for Davy's reinstatement go through in time. There is much to be done there, and we find little pleasure in some of the prospect, although to have a home again, and to be in that beautiful country, will be really heavenly. They won't be able to transfer Davy for several months, so we will be able to relax and try to make definite accomplishments there. It is going to be interesting to know what the new year may bring. . . .

Wupatki
April 19, 1946

Dear M.,

. . . As you see, we're at Wupatki. Davy came out here the first of January; I was recuperating from pneumonia, and didn't come out till the first of February. There had been no firewood brought in here, so I came out with the firewood, and all has been wonderful ever since. It was so good to get back, and we are enjoying every moment. The place was the most gosh-awful mess, but it has kept us so busy that we haven't had time to think about much else, and it is good to see things beginning to look nice. Davy has to spend most of every day on cleaning up stuff, but he is getting it all beautifully organized, and we are about to start the annual sign painting. He also plastered the dining room and painted it and our kitchen, so we have two lovely fresh rooms, which adds much to our morale.

Davy wants a transfer, wanted it badly right at first, but now we have gotten up the old interest and don't mind at all when they say it won't come for a year or so. There isn't any place as beautiful as Wupatki as far as we are concerned, but Davy wants to get some other experience. I guess we hit a real low when we came back, because Davy seriously considered quitting the NPS, but if they will run it the way he wants them to he will make it his career. He had the management of two good trading posts offered to him, but when it came right down to quitting, things looked better here! . . .

Jimmy Brewer is back at Navajo. He and Sallie are divorced at last, and she is still at Tumacacori, where Earl Jackson is now custodian. . . . Everyone has more visitors than ever before. The Canyon is averaging over a thousand a day, and we are having as many as in the middle of summer. It is going to be ghastly in a couple of months unless they can give us some help. And our roads are worse than they have ever been. . . .

Very little of our garden survived our absence—no lawn, and we are waiting for the summer rains to start it. Of course if we had known we would have April showers we could have done something with it—it has been raining off and on for over a week and has been simply marvellous. Our native shrubs are magnificent now though—had to be pruned like anything, and have already bloomed—also I

have put in many wild plants this spring, but it is too soon
to know what will take hold. Phil's mother planted us two
wild four o'clocks and they are growing beautifully and
have buds, so that looks very promising. Time flies so fast
it is hard to keep up with all the things and it's already too
late to do all the transplanting I'd planned—but it is fun to
see things get started.

Davy goes to Zion [National Park] to fire school next
week. . . . They don't take wives to fire school—it is
strictly stag—but I'm glad he will have a chance to see
Zion and they will also go up to Bryce [Canyon National
Park] when school is over. . . . I'm supposed to be writing a
book on modern Navajo rugs, but sometimes I wonder if
that was a smart idea.

Davy has been writing like mad for a week—he got
word that the *Arizona Highways* wanted an issue on national
monuments, and the fellows could get paid if they could
turn out their articles in a week. Since he had to do both
Sunset and Wupatki it has kept him tearing his hair, but it
is finished now, and we hope it will be O.K. . . .

Well, it is time to do something with the bread I'm making. I want to make a cake today too—tomorrow is our
eighth anniversary, and the first time in three years we
have been together for the event! . . .

Wupatki
May 12, 1946

Dear Marian,

. . . Mr. Buchenberg is back, my boarder, the man who
lived in the trailer out here and worked on ways to fix up
the ruins. He is busy at work again, going over the tests he
and Davy made, and is paying me $15 a week for his
meals, which is very generous and I will be able to save a

lot of it. I am putting it in Postal Savings so it is separate from our savings account, and plan to use it for a vacuum cleaner if we ever have electricity. He got here the day before Davy returned from Fire School. . . .

Our kitty has gone away or been eaten by an owl. She isn't at the Peshlakais', and one of their cats is missing too. Alas. Now we have a packrat digging a hole through the wall in the bedroom and are trying vainly to trap it. Everything in the yard grew beautifully while we had the cat— our wild four o'clocks have from 19 to 25 flowers each and every afternoon—bright magenta.

Did I tell you about the Peshlakai family fight? Sally and Clyde had an awful battle and she left for a week. It is all settled now. I think she will get a separate permit for her own sheep, as he got bossy and said he owned all of them, as he held the family permit. They seem quite happy and are all living in a tent at Heiser Spring.

There is a movie being made at Cameron and every Navajo with a wagon and team is going down, as they pay $25.00 a day for a man with such equipment. We won't have a Navajo on the place and I bet we can never hire them again.

Wupatki
late August 1946

Dear M.,

. . . Our Navajos had some Squaw Dances about a month ago and we went to three within a week. We were invited to some of the daytime ceremonies and of course that was the really exciting part. The first night the dance was on the monument; we went down at 10:30 when we had put our groceries away, after the weekly trip to town. The dance didn't start until about 1:30 a.m. because long talks were given by some of the council delegates about what the Navajo Council was doing, and what had gone on during a recent trip to Washington, and a final pep talk about how they should have a good time, but not get too drunk and spoil the dances for other people. We watched for a while, then went to sleep. It was nice to lie there in the warm evening (morning) and listen to the singing. At dawn the dance began to break up and the people got into their wagons and trucks and went over to Clyde's farm where that day's ceremony was to be.

We went over too, and were invited right in to break-fast: boiled mutton and that flat bread, and coffee. After we ate all we could hold (it really was good) they brought in a second course: fried bread and roast mutton ribs, both of which are the best the Navajos cook, so we ate again. We sat on the floor around a tarp, with the best friends of the family, and felt quite honored. When we all finished, we left the hogan and a second batch of guests went in to take our places. That went on all day; in fact, the families giving the Sing had to feed around two hundred people, and everyone ate about half the time.

Sally and Catherine had about six women helping them cook on the campfire, and it was interesting to see prac-tically an assembly line—sheep being slain and skinned and cut up on one end, and a steady stream of bowls and pans of food going into the hogan at the other. We were glad we were among the first, as the cooks got a little ahead of the diners and we saw them later stacking bread and hunks of cooked mutton in big cardboard cartons, which didn't look so appetizing.

By the time we were through the sun was up and the ceremony was to begin, so we went up on a hill. The camp was in a little valley, surrounded by rolling hills, with the river in the background. The ceremonial procession, headed by a girl on horseback, carrying the banner (War Dance trophy, should have a fresh scalp), and consisting of wagons and people on horses, came out of one of the canyons and started to the middle of the valley.[30] The hosts of the day sent out a party of boys on horseback to greet them, and they rode round and round the valley, whooping and yipping like coyotes, and it was even more exciting when two old men began firing guns.

Everything quieted down in a few minutes, and they all got off their horses and began to put up a shelter for the guests—built it out of branches and green sticks in just a short time. There was also to be a ceremonial exchange of gifts, but we all missed it. They are very definite about time, telling you the exact hour, but often they get the numbers confused, so they say eight o'clock when they mean four, etc. We didn't get to see the curing ceremony, but were on hand when the victims, I mean the patients, came out—they were blackened, and wore blankets and had feathers in their hair.

At the dance that night we had some of the Navajos sitting with us, and were amused that they would make the same comments about the couples that we would make. Everybody was enjoying the fact that one of the patients, Clark Smith, made a quick recovery and danced every dance.

The encampment was simply beautiful—I have never seen such color. There by the river it is rather drab country, but it made a lovely setting for all the wagons and horses, and all the happy people in their best clothes. You know they had to preserve their pre-war clothing carefully, since plush and velveteen haven't been available, but every dress and shirt looked new and shiny, and they all wore simply pounds of jewelry.

The Caywoods [custodians at Walnut Canyon] were out, camping with their two children near the Trading Post, and there were three boys from Grand Canyon, but that was all the white people. Davy was prepared for many

dances and was simply loaded with change, but he and
Louis Caywood fell asleep when the dance started and the
little girls were too shy to wake them up. . . .

A lot has happened this year—after a slow start, things
have moved quickly and they are treating custodians like
kings—it feels almost as good as when we had the Boss. We
have a ranger here, and one at Sunset Crater, and they are
trying to get a bunch of bulldozers and stuff to work on the
roads, and everything is really getting in good shape. . . .

Wupatki
April 5, 1947

Dear Lizzie B,

. . . Our Navajos have been having a Sing, but we didn't
go, being a little too busy here. Modesta, the sister of Sally
and Catherine, who talks good English, has been visiting
them and she comes over and talks to me quite often. She's
quite interesting, and I like to hear her reactions to living in
a hogan and taking care of sheep—it's practically new to
her as she has lived in a town for so long. Her eight children
are being educated in public schools, which is good for
them, but in a way I think she is wrong not to have them
learn Navajo, for they would have a better chance to get
really good jobs with the Indian Service or some other kind
of work on the reservation where they could do some good
for their own people. They know hardly any Navajo. . . .

Wupatki
April 19, 1947

Dear Marian,

. . . Guess I hadn't told you we do have [the lights]
installed—nearly—anyway, the last two evenings have
been simply heavenly. I knew I put off doing lots of things

Courtney and Modesta Dixon (sister of Sally and Catherine Peshlakai) sewing on "the porch" (Photograph by Tad Nichols)

in the evenings because it was too hard to carry a lamp into another room with my hands full, and open and shut doors and get stuff out to work on—so now, for the first time since we first came to Wupatki, I was able to put the laundry away after dark. And I dawdled over the dishes because it was so nice to be able to see them clearly and put them away. We have especially good lighting in the kitchen—a fluorescent one over the stove, and a regular 100w fixture over the sink. We still have no lamps except my little copper one, but Davy took the shade off one of the gas lamps and put a bulb under it with a long cord so we can hang it over the desk or chairs temporarily. We have two lamp bases cut out and ready to carve, and will probably make our own shade frames, as we can't get the rectangular shape we want. Last night I was able to work on one of the end tables out in the garage, with plenty of light. We finished one last week, and the other will be done by Monday. It is a relief to get some of our projects done. . . .

We are enjoying life here more than usual, I think, and we often wonder why. For one thing, it is such a blessing not to get a headache in town and to feel so rotten that I can't really enjoy an evening of visiting, and then dread the trip home so much—maybe that affected Davy, too—anyway, we haven't been getting home from town till anywhere from eleven, at the earliest, to two a.m., and don't worry about it at all. . . . Sometimes I eat with other girls in town, but Sarah [Hubert] is so interesting I really enjoy being with her more. It seems like some of the girls in town get in a rut of cleaning the house with the vacuum every day and never read or do anything amusing, or know anything about the country—you know the kind—the ones who practically make their kids take off their shoes to come in the house.

The girl who has been sewing for me is wonderful, and

we visit her and her husband often—they are really alert—her house is kind of dilapidated, but her children are so happy, and she is happy, and they let the unimportant things go. I've read so many articles lately about women being too busy keeping their houses nice to have fun with their children, and find the ones who do have fun with their children are the most interesting in other ways, too. . . .

. . . [Davy] got an "Excellent" rating this time, which is tops, and means he will have a good chance at any job he wants. Also it is good compensation for what I think has been the hardest year he has ever put in—so many interruptions and so much just repair for all the depreciation that went on during the war—and yet he has gotten more for the monument in the way of improvements than in all the time before. We are more ready to leave here now that he has gotten things caught up. He gets quite excited about some of the jobs that come up and will probably start applying for some of them. Of course, they circulate the field and it means hundreds of applicants, but he has heard of one or two which would really be interesting and help him get the experience he wants. He heard of one in Alaska which is a keen job, but has decided not to apply, as it is too much like the Wupatki job, and doesn't offer the chance to work with many more people.

(next day)
Sunday, April 20th
9th Wedding Anniversary
. . . I forgot to tell you about the Peshlakais and some others who had a Sing about two weeks ago, and we got to see one of the sandpaintings. We were invited to see all of them but every day something else came up and we didn't get there. That will be one fine reason to have a car, because I could go when Davy was busy.

The sandpainting we saw was a dilly—four tall people, black, white, blue, and yellow, with lots of snakes all over them. We asked if we could stay for the ceremony and they said Bea[31] and I could stay but they didn't want any men, as Sally and Theresa had to take off their blouses and would feel embarrassed. So Bea and I stayed, and Hal Smith was medicine man, and we watched him sprinkle the painting with pollen and say the prayers, and then he had Sally and Theresa walk into it and sit down on it during the singing. After the singing, he sang little prayers and picked up the sand and rubbed it on them, on their feet, legs, shoulders, arms and heads. When they were all through, they swept up the sandpainting and carried it out. During part of it they served medicine, but luckily they didn't offer us any nor spit it in our faces, and they burned some kind of herbs and the women sat in the smoke and rubbed it on themselves. . . .

Wupatki
June 30, 1947

Dear Lizzie B.,

I still can't get over my trip, and keep thinking about it all the time. The greenery just overwhelmed me, to see trees completely covering the streets and green out of every window. I was afraid I wouldn't like Wupatki when I got back, but of course, I do. Even with the dust storms which we have every other day.

Have kept very busy since I got home—painted the drainboard this last week, which caused no end of inconvenience. Now I am going to start painting the walls with some old coldwater paint—it will make them look fresh and clean at least, and if Vergil Tso[32] stays out here, we will hire him to help. He has been working on a farm near town and has all sorts of fine cowboy clothes and also bought a horse and a bicycle! . . .

Wupatki
July 6, 1947

Dear Liz,

   . . . All the time we were painting we had company, of course . . . No place to stay in town as the Pow-Wow was on. We even went to it yesterday. After dinner we got dressed up and went in to the Hopi Exhibit at the Museum, then to dinner with friends, and to the evening ceremonial dances, and stayed all night. I just wish we had all of you to see the Ceremonials—it is really quite wonderful—after dark, out in the city park where the Indians camp, and they have a grandstand, with four huge bonfires. They have Indians come from all over—Kiowas, Arapahoes, Comanches, Zunis, and of course, lots of Hopis and Navajos. All put on their show dances with feathered costumes, and the grand finale is a Navajo Fire Dance—they come out in the dark and get firebrands from the bonfires and chase each other and whoop and sing, and it is very exciting. The most fun, of course, is to go around the Indian encampment and watch them trade with the dudes, and then watch them riding the tilt-a-whirl, etc. at the Carnival. . . .

   Did I tell you Davy and I are going to adopt a baby? Waited to tell anyone till they got all the papers made out, and investigations finished, and now I forgot whether I told you. Started in January and it will probably be several months yet. The County does the investigations and surely is thorough in asking all kinds of questions—they have very strict laws now on account of that "black market" situation, and it is a good thing. Since we may get one up to two years old, I am not making any preparations till we know how old it will be.

Dear Lizzie B.,

. . . Sally Peshlakai finally left Clyde—whether permanently or not, we do not know. She came over one day last week in much distress and talked it over with us, and Vergil, who was here working at the time. She finally decided to go to Gray Mountain and stay with some relatives, and Davy went with her back to the hogan to get her clothes. He tried to get Clyde to loan her the wagon for the trip, but Clyde was obstinate, so Davy took her to Flag (he had to go in anyway) and she was going to get a ride from there. Later he saw her when he came through Gray Mountain on his way from taking some people to Tonalea, and said she looked very well and happy. I shall miss her something terrible. We had her and Vergil to lunch that day, and it was quite an ordeal for all. I guess everyone around here is going to miss her. Sally is going to have to go to the Navajo Court in Tuba City to try to get some sheep—the family has eaten hers, or something—anyway, she doesn't have any to take with her, and no wool to weave with. It will all straighten out, but it is quite sad.

Dear Folksies and Sisters,

So far Labor Day weekend hasn't flooded us with the ordinary visities—but, oh, last week, and the crowds—

Clyde Peshlakai and Mady Fleming (Photograph by Rex Fleming)

thank goodness for a very good ranger who guided almost
incessantly. The main thing has been our company, keeping us busy. Rex and Mady Fleming, he's a photographer,
were here, and Davy just about devoted his time to getting
them around the country since Rex is making a movie of
the monument. They are grand people, and we spent most
of every day out wandering around and eating at weird
times—went to Grand Falls on the Little Colorado, which
is bigger than Niagara, and was running full. The spray
from it is red dust, and we were quite a sight after spending
a morning clambering around the canyon and taking pictures from all angles. . . .

Well, August has passed without our knowing any more about either our baby or the car, but perhaps we were a little over-eager, and at least have been so busy we haven't been worrying. . . . We have several good books on child care, and are waiting to read others when we are more sure what age child we will have. There seems to be a little question about the one we were considering, although we will know more about it in a few days. . . .

You asked whether we would keep Mr. B—we have had some sessions about that, and think we will let our decision ride till we see how we make out. As it happens, he will be away probably from October first till the first of January, so if we get the baby this fall, we would have plenty of time to get adjusted to the schedule, and see whether it would be too much work to keep boarding him. Actually, he is wonderfully adaptable, and this week of tearing around and eating all sorts of food at any time hasn't bothered him or us a bit, so I know he wouldn't mind a bit of confusion. If by any chance we get a child over a year old, I'm sure he would leave of his own accord, since he is not accustomed to kids, and when his daughter and her family were here with us for two days a couple of weeks ago, he was a wreck because the children made him nervous—and we thought they were remarkably quiet and well behaved! . . . Isn't it nice we have the lovely patio where we can put the baby in the sun even during the winter? If we get a little baby we will get to name it, but I suppose the older ones come complete with someone else's choice. . . .

Grandmother Peshlakai, Clyde's mother, died on Wednesday. Davy & Danny went over to bury her. Estimates of her age varied from 96 to 102, and she looked every minute of it. I imagine it is a relief to the girl who was taking care of her, since she had to be carried around during the last year, and was almost completely helpless—

which is pretty tough when you live in a hogan. Incidentally, Sally Peshlakai is back among the family—Rex, Mady & I walked over there yesterday morning, and all looked very happy and contented.

Wupatki
November 12, 1947

Dear M.—

Janie's a cherub in her pink sweater—so very soft and such a good design—only those who've dressed babies could realize how "knitted-in" sleeves excel. Did *you* make it with such speed? . . . We may have pictures eventually. As yet, she looks just like a baby—but she has a most endearing smile and uses it all the time.

Fires in the wood stove and fireplace lately, for a cozy feeling and nice seasonal juniper smell. We have a car at last—a Ford sedan-coupe which is just right. We took Janie with us yesterday to trading posts in the vicinity to track down the extent of an earthquake we felt recently. Wouldn't a nice tame volcano be fun to watch? The local volcanic field is only dormant—"they" think.

We're the proudest parents and Janie is darling. Wupatki looks better with diapers on the line.

Wupatki
November 21, 1947

Dear M. and Mother—

You *dear* people—Janie's little fork and spoon are the loveliest we've ever seen—and she will love them dearly. It is such a joy to have nice things for our little baby. She's the nicest thing in our lives. I don't think there's ever been an instant we haven't felt she is our very own—but in many ways we feel such a responsibility toward her. She came to us with the sweetest, happiest disposition, that we especially want to help her keep. It is interesting to see what lovely surprises she has in her own personality, and to think of what we shall want to help her develop for happiness all her life.

She's developing *our* personalities, as Davy said the other day. "No matter how worried or frustrated I feel, it always makes me feel wonderful to go look at Janie and watch her smile and laugh."

I keep her with me in her basket while I work around the house. When dire things happen in the kitchen, she's always there, laughing serenely. She's a doll-baby in the little sweater—and I've just realized it is peach-color, which is more becoming to Janie than the usual pink. She's propped on a pillow at the moment, rattling her rattle and shouting with joy. I'm afraid I'm a *very* doting mama!

We have lovely snow coming down—my grandmother used to say, "someone is shaking a featherbed"—the desert is alternately obliterated and shining. . . . I wish we could stay here and raise Janie at Wupatki; but wherever we are we will try to teach her to love the country. That's the one unchanging thing.

Our Navajos are so interested in her, they are coming in often—mostly it's just to *look*, but Susie Lee picked her up and cuddled her and talked baby-talk Navajo to her.

Wupatki
December 20, 1947

Dear M.—

Christmas comes apace and I'm just dashing this off before Janie's feeding. We want you to know your present this year is not only a box of food to England, but also part of a

Courtney, Janie, and Davy Jones by the fireplace of the new
house at Wupatki, Christmas 1947 (Photograph by Rex Fleming)

Navajo Christmas party! The party is Monday, and *how* we
wish you could attend—such festivities have not been in-
dulged in at Wupatki before—but this is going to be a
Christmas they'll remember. Our Navajos aren't quite as im-
poverished as some; their standard of living was low to begin with—but the kids do love a tree & candy & toys & the

adults do too. Along with the fun we'll have boxes of relief
supplies—but the most thing is the party & tree, as most of
the children here have never seen any such thing. . . .

Wupatki
January 5, 1948

Dear M.—

. . . Will try to get a clipping about *the party* for you.
The Flemings did the nicest thing we've ever heard of—
hand-picked the relief goods; Mady washed from 10 to 15
tubs of clothing a day for a couple of weeks so they would
be clean. If you hear any scandal about the relief goods,
don't blame anyone for dumping the high-heeled shoes
and bathing suits. The Flemings also took three trailer
loads out into the real backwoods and sought out the desti-
tute families who could not get to relief distribution centers. It was the most unselfish and generous evidence of
true Christmas spirit we've ever seen. They came in as visitors a year ago and are a very nice young couple—he's a
photographer. They certainly fit in at Wupatki.

Excuse incoherencies due to last night's fire dance. The
dream of many years was realized and it was more wonderful than words could tell. All best wishes for the New Year.

Wupatki
March 29, 1948

Dear Folksies & Sisters,

It isn't often that most of the laundry is dry, formula
made, Janie bathed & asleep by 10:15 a.m., but somehow
we got off to a good start. Mr. B. is back, and as a rule we
are lagging behind schedule, but he was anxious to get to
town this morning. As to the dry laundry—that is thanks

to about a 70 mph wind, and the diapers are a delicate
pink from dust. Not that they haven't been pink lately
anyway—Davy has done work on the spring, and our water has been a little thick lately. . . .

The spring is working beautifully now—Janie & I went
over to look, and they have a terrific trench about nine feet
deep with water running out the end in a good stream.
They dug down through the rock with an air compressor &
jackhammer, and everyone was certainly covered with
mud. They would get so tired us girls would fix coffee &
lunches between meals for them, but that part is over and
now all they have to do is cover the trench. Davy is going
to put the Quonset hut up above the spring, and hopes to
get the temporary ranger's apartment in it done before we
get a temporary ranger. I don't quite see how he is going to
manage to go to Santa Barbara to work on the movie with
Rex [Fleming] in April, but we still plan to do that.

Catherine Peshlakai is expecting a baby in April, and
they had quite a time getting anyone lined up to stay with
her & help with the work, what with this being lambing
time, and shearing coming up; however, Modesta and three
of her youngest children arrived a week ago, and will stay
unless everyone gets in a fight before then. . . .

Wupatki
May 14, 1948

Dear M.—

. . . So you've had your christening! Aren't the babies
wonderful? Janie hasn't been christened—I wanted to have
it done at Tuba City while the folks were here, but Davy
won't go into a church if it isn't pretty and churchlike, so
we slide along. Janie's a terror—she doesn't exactly crawl

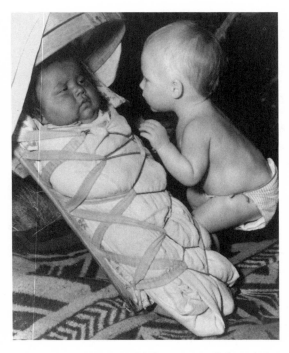

Janie Jones and Ray Peshlakai in a cradleboard, August 1948
(Photograph by Rex Fleming)

but moves like lightning, somewhat in the style of an inch-
worm, pulling with her arms and pushing with one toe—up
the stone steps and all over. We spend the cooler part of
the morning in the patio, where she consumes clover, sand,
rocks, sticks, etc. She uses us as a jungle gym, climbs up our
legs into our laps. Wears diapers and soakers and seldom
anything else, as it's like dressing a tiger. She still has the
angelic disposition and happily laughs and sings all day.
She doesn't seem like any extra work—I probably had too
much spare time! Mother says she just can't believe Janie
isn't our own, as she reminds her of me at that age. . . .

Wupatki
May 17, 1948

Dear M.—

. . . Davy is such a wonderful Daddy. We take turns getting Janie up and giving her breakfast, and he's always
coming around at bathtime when he can. I really couldn't
manage the whole business if he weren't so eager to help.
He spent Mother's Day trying to teach her to say "Mom-
mie," but she just chortles "Da-da!"

Wupatki
March 7, 1949

Dear M.,

. . . The monument personnel are being dispersed—Paul
Beaubien of Walnut to Omaha! And other moves, all over.
We may be included, but as Davy says in his idealistic/realis-
tic way: you can't get back where you want to be unless you
get out and work up to the top—reminds me of Churchill in
the new book—it's a wonderful thing to have all the power
you need when you know what to do & how to do it. I'm interested to see if the old custodians who worked under the
Boss make any kind of a splash when they go out into other
parts of the Service. Thank goodness, they may keep us in
the Southwest—at least that's the rumor—you know the
grapevine was always more reliable than official word. . . .

Wupatki
June 12, 1949

Dear folks,

. . . It is already a happy birthday. We are having *rain*,
the Janie doll is smarter & cuter every day, and yesterday

Janie Jones in a Navajo dress made by Sally Peshlakai, and moccasins made by Courtney, August 1948 (Photograph by Rex Fleming)

Davy received an award of $100 (!) from the Interior Department for his cut-out letter sign suggestion! . . .

Janie is getting rarer & rarer. She has to "get in bed by the self" now, also insists on putting on her dresses, etc. . . . She can climb all the ladders in the ruin alone, which just petrifies the visitors, but we have to help her get down. . . . She helped me with the washing this morning, and we ended up with the washing about two-thirds done in time for a late lunch, and Janie had had two baths and five changes of clothing. . . .

Courtney, Davy, and Janie (in moccasins) outside the new house, 1949 (Photograph by Tad Nichols)

Wupatki
August 3, 1949

Dear M.,

Could you please send us an outline of Hannah's feet? Posthaste? Janie has finally found a reliable source of miniature Navajo moccasins and we want Hannah to have some. . . . We have raised Janie in "moccys" and bare feet and are much enthused with the results. . . .

Have thought of you so much—but I have so much "help" with everything (including this letter) that I generally end up on the floor playing rather than writing.

Davy has applied for what we think is the perfect job—superintendent of a new national monument in Puerto Rico—sounds almost too good to be true, as it would be another chance to "pioneer" before the desk jobs close in. Can hardly stand the suspense for he's so enthusiastic about the possibilities. Meanwhile Wupatki is wonderful and we're taking advantage of some rain to get a lawn started. . . .

Afterword

Courtney Reeder Jones

I returned to Wupatki in the fall of 1988, taking along my friend Lisa Rappoport to drive and take photographs. I had been invited by the superintendent, Larry Henderson, who was restoring the beautiful stone house built by the Civilian Conservation Corps (CCC) at Wupatki as the Park Service residence. It was the fiftieth anniversary of the CCC, and the house had become a "historic building." Davy and I had been its first tenants.

On that classically beautiful afternoon in October, we turned off Highway 89, north of Flagstaff, on the now-surfaced road through the black cinders to Sunset Crater. We came upon an unobtrusive visitor's center in the forest with a large parking space, and there were many cars. We visited the privy, which was painted black inside, and then hastened on toward Wupatki, flying over a paved road, now unimpeded by chunks of lava and deep holes. It was not like my first trip to Wupatki in Paul Beaubien's rattling green Park Service truck!

We came out of the forest and black cinders into rolling land where views of the far rosy cliffs of the Painted Desert are framed by cinder hills in shades of plum and gray. Huge clumps of chrome-yellow rabbit brush were still blooming. When Lisa began exclaiming, "How good it smells!" I realized that the golden buckwheat was also in bloom. Farther along in Wupatki Basin the ground became

Courtney at Wupatki, 1988 (Photograph by Lisa Rappoport)

red, and slabs of Moenkopi sandstone stuck out from drifts of cinders.

I had begun looking for my favorite ruin, Wukoki, when we saw it proclaimed by a sign and a surfaced road leading toward it. Then there was Wupatki, or rather the monument visitor's center with its parking lot, signs, drinking fountains, and restrooms. We could not see the ruin itself until we passed through the building. Then we had our first view of it, far enough away not to be dominated by the park facilities. It stands on its own peninsula, glowing and independent.

Our once-solitary stone house, now being restored, had assumed its proper place in the landscape, diminished by the visitor's center, as had been intended, as well as by a huge cottonwood tree and two rows of apartment buildings. We settled into a furnished apartment, unpacked, and had a little supper. Lisa took her sleeping bag and went to spend the night at Wukoki.

In the morning, I went to watch the sun rise over the Hopi Buttes near Winslow. I found a surfaced path around "our ruin," with little markers for use with a self-guiding leaflet. The texture of the rock work had been changed by stabilization, and the restored rooms where we once lived had been demolished.

After breakfast, we went to the old storage building where Davy's office had been. Lisa examined photo files while I poked through collections for evidence of our twelve-year residence at the site. No luck; the slate was clean. The Park Service personnel gave me the opportunity to talk extensively, and videotaped my reminiscences about the olden days.

On a second trip, Larry and Signe Henderson took me to Wupatki in June 1990, just before they left the post. I was their guest in the superintendent's residence at Heiser Springs. The springs had been used to water the Navajos' flocks; I don't know how they are used now. There are wells that provide enough water for several residences with their washing machines, but there are no sheep. The breathtaking June heat, and the far cliffs of the Painted Desert, shimmering through the heat waves, were overwhelming, and I became sick.

When I recovered, the chief ranger, Anna Fender, took me sightseeing in an air-conditioned car. We swooped out to Highway 89 on the "new road." It had been surveyed in our time. On the pass between the Doney Peaks, a picnic

area takes advantage of the view, and a smooth path leads
to the top of the hill. The sharp and chunky terrain up
there used to be littered with volcanic bombs, spindle,
breadcrust, etc. I don't remember seeing them this time.

The Citadel loomed over its sink where the eagles
nested. Lomaki and Box Canyon ruin (is that our Ruin J?),
once so lonely in the midst of great rolling grasslands, are
now neatly stabilized and furnished with their own little
roads and trails. Stabilization does wonders for the preser-
vation of ruins, but they used to look so much more picturesque. Long ago on a bitter winter day, we found in the
box canyon the cold remains of a fire and, on a ledge, the
partly-roasted remains of a horse.

That summer, I went back to Wupatki a third time, in
my son-in-law's air-conditioned pickup. I had given ad-
vance notice to my Navajo friends, the three sisters Sally,
Catherine, and Modesta, two of whom had been married
to Clyde Peshlakai. We visited them in their neat wooden
houses across the river; they had been moved off the
monument by the Park Service after we left. With me was
my daughter Janie, who had climbed the ladders at Wupatki when she was two years old and played in the hogans
and cuddled the baby lambs. Janie's daughter, Felicity, was
along, too. She enjoyed hearing the soft Navajo language
when our ranger/interpreter/guide, Inez Paddock, yelled it
into my dear friend Sally's ear. We felt lucky to have Inez
with us; she is related to everybody.

I am going to return to Wupatki again next spring with
Lisa. I hope Inez can take us to visit the other old friends
that I missed on this visit. I still dream of sitting under a
tree, spinning wool with the Navajo ladies and looking out
over the desert.

Notes

Introduction

1. Peter J. Pilles, Jr., "The Sinagua: Ancient People of the Flagstaff Region," in *Exploration: Annual Bulletin of the School of American Research* (1987): 7.
2. Bruce A. Anderson, "Wupatki National Monument: Exploring into Prehistory," in *Exploration* (1987): 18.
3. Scott Thybony, *Fire and Stone* (Tucson, Ariz.: Southwest Parks and Monuments Association, 1987), pp. 16, 20–21.
4. Ibid., p. 32.
5. Anderson, "Wupatki," pp. 18–19.
6. Robert H. Lister and Florence C. Lister, *Those Who Came Before* (Globe, Ariz.: Southwest Parks and Monuments Association, 1983), p. 177.
7. Thybony, *Fire and Stone*, p. 33.
8. Ibid., p. 9.
9. Marilyn Taylor, "Time Traveling to Crack-in-Rock," *Arizona Highways* (June 1992): 44.
10. Thybony, *Fire and Stone*, pp. 31–32.
11. Lister and Lister, *Those Who Came Before*, p. 177.
12. Sallie Pierce Brewer, "The 'Long Walk' to Bosque Redondo, as told by Peshlakai Etsedi," in *Museum Notes of the Museum of Northern Arizona* (May 1937): 56.
13. Raymond Friday Locke, *The Book of the Navajo* (Los Angeles: Mankind Publishing, 1992), pp. 346–49.
14. Alexandra Roberts, "Navajo Ethno-History and Archeology," chap. 6 in *The Wupatki Archeological Inventory Survey Project:*

Final Report (Santa Fe, N.M.: National Park Service, 1990), pp. 9–10.

15. Alexandra Roberts, "The Wupatki Navajos: An Historical Sketch," in *Exploration* (1987): 29.

16. Roberts, "Navajo Ethno-History and Archeology," p. 10.

17. Ibid., p. 20.

18. Ibid., pp. 22–24.

Letters from Wupatki

1. Tad Nichols, a photographer and filmmaker, and Mary Jane, his wife, were friends from the University of Arizona. They later built a house in Tucson at the edge of the Catalina Mountains. Courtney, Davy, the Nichols, and M. all met on a field trip excavating the Kinishba ruin in the White Mountains.

2. Each of the National Park Service (NPS) custodians (later called superintendents) had to file a report every month, which was published in the *Southwestern Monuments Monthly Narrative Reports* and avidly read by the twenty-seven others.

3. Sally Peshlakai taught Courtney to spin, dye, and weave in the Navajo style. Courtney wrote an unpublished article on Navajo weaving and a shorter article about Sally, "A Navajo Weaver in Her Home," published in the *Pow-Wow Program* in 1940.

4. Dr. Harold S. Colton founded the Museum of Northern Arizona in 1926. He was a zoologist and archaeologist, and his wife, Mary Russell F. Colton, was interested in ethnology and Indian art.

5. Milton Wetherill was in charge of Navajo National Monument part-time before the Brewers took over. In the 1880s, Milton's father and uncles were the first white people to discover the Mesa Verde cliff houses in the southwestern corner of Colorado near the town of Cortez. Milton's uncle John Wetherill was the first custodian of Navajo National Monument.

6. Jimmy and Sallie Brewer, the first full-time custodians of Wupatki (from 1934 to 1936), became custodians of Navajo National Monument in 1937. Betatakin and Keet Seel are the best-known ruins at the monument, located in northeastern Arizona near Kayenta.

7. Katharine Bartlett, a historian from the University of Denver, was the head librarian and assistant to Dr. Colton at the Museum of Northern Arizona. She now lives in Sedona, Arizona.

8. Sally was married to Clyde Peshlakai, the head of the Wupatki Basin Navajo group. He also married her sister Catherine, as was the custom. Sally later divorced Clyde and married Emmett Lee, who was also a son of Peshlakai Etsidi and thus Clyde's half-brother. Because Emmett's (and Hal Smith's) mother was Clyde's half-sister by marriage, both men were also Clyde's nephews.

9. The *Christian Science Monitor* published Courtney's article "Life in a Ruin" on July 24, 1940, with photographs by Tad Nichols.

10. Beaubien, an archaeologist from the University of Denver with extensive experience in the western United States, was the first ranger at Walnut Canyon National Monument (east of Flagstaff) when it was transferred from the U.S. Forest Service to the NPS in 1934. He made the telephone in his Forest Service cabin available to all the custodians and later helped the Joneses with nightly radio phone contact.

11. When the manager of the Monte Vista Hotel restaurant criticized the Joneses for bringing a Navajo into the café, Davy told him, "It is better to bring a nice, clean Navajo into your café than to allow movie stars to take their horses upstairs in the elevator," which was actually happening.

12. Hugh Miller had previously been the assistant superintendent of the Southwest National Monuments.

13. "The Boss" was Frank Pinkley, superintendent of the Southwest National Monument's twenty-eight "lone posts," most of which were cared for by only a single custodian and, if married, his wife. Pinkley, who was well loved by the custodians, had recently died.

14. Courtney's article "A Navajo Weaver in Her Home" was published in *Pow-Wow Program*, Flagstaff, Arizona, 1940.

15. Jimmy Kaywanwytewa, a Hopi, worked for the Museum of Northern Arizona as a caretaker and interpreter. He made a complete set of beautiful kachina dolls in the old style for the museum.

16. Don Egermeyer was chief ranger at Casa Grande Ruins National Monument near Phoenix, and then at Saguaro National Monument outside Tucson.

17. The Wilders were good friends from the University of Arizona. Judith was a botanist, and Carleton was an ethnologist who later did social work. Carleton was a ranger naturalist at the Grand Canyon and then at Saguaro National Monument.

18. The Coles used to visit from California. Butler was a cabinetmaker and teacher of cabinetry; Lee helped Courtney with knitting.

19. Mr. Buchenburg worked on stabilizing and restoring some of the ruins at Wupatki and Casa Grande on his own initiative and without financial backing. However, the four-story structure at Casa Grande Ruins National Monument is still protected from rain by the modern roof that Mr. Buchenburg hoped would someday be removed.

20. Archaeologists believe the Sinagua of Wupatki adopted the use of ballcourts for games with religious connotations from the Hohokam (Lister and Lister, *Those Who Came Before*, pp. 37, 105).

21. A Navajo Sing is a religious ceremony (*hataal*, formerly translated "holy chant" or "song," is now more commonly translated "way") intended to keep people in harmony with the universe. The singer is called a *Hataali*, generally translated as "medicine man" (Locke, *Book of the Navajo*, p. 47).

22. Mr. and Mrs. Edgar M. Craven were visitors the first year the Joneses were at Wupatki, and they returned as friends each year thereafter. They always invited Courtney and Davy to dinner at the Grand Canyon, but the Joneses generally could not accept because they had only the Park Service truck, so it was a special treat to go with Mr. Buchenburg in his car.

23. Hal Smith, Clyde's half-brother and nephew (see note 8). ("Peshlakai" means "smith.")

24. Jimmy Brewer gave this nickname to Nez ka Yazzie, the medicine man, because Jimmy said he would make "a grand post." His Navajo name means "little fat man."

25. Al Whiting was an ethnobotanist who worked at the Museum of Northern Arizona and taught at Dartmouth College.

26. Philip van Cleave came from the University of Illinois as a dollar-a-day roustabout. During the war, and the Joneses' absence, he was the ranger in charge of Wupatki.

27. The Hopi Craftsman show began a few years after the Navajo Craftsman to encourage the production and display of traditional Native American crafts such as weaving, leather work, and the making of silver jewelry, baskets, and pottery. Jimmy and Sallie Brewer initially proposed the idea of an exhibit in 1936 as a way to preserve traditional Navajo arts. The first Navajo Craftsman Exhibition opened June 6, 1936, near Wupatki. The Coltons of the Museum of Northern Arizona helped greatly with both of these yearly exhibits (Roberts, "Navajo Ethno-History and Archaeology," pp. 17–19).

28. Sandpaintings, made with different colored sand, corn-meal, flower pollen, powdered roots, stone, and bark, are an essential part of most Navajo ceremonies (Locke, *Book of the Navajo*, p. 50).

29. Courtney's article "Spindle-Spinning: Navajo Style" was published in *Plateau*, January 1946.

30. This ceremony was given to honor the Navajos who had been in the war. Many from the Wupatki area were killed in the South Pacific.

31. Bea and Bob Upton came from Chicago. Bob was the first ranger at Wupatki while Davy remained custodian, now called superintendent.

32. Vergil Tso was Sally Peshlakai's son by an earlier marriage.

practical.
... ert at Chas +
... ry one asked

... k to Coolidge
... t as Davy
... e next eve
... for supper +
... that night —
... aved a lot
... s the scenery
... g here today!
... ery thrilling
... me settle down.
... m yesterday

...ayed at Paul's all night had
...ner at Colton's - everyone who was
...he meeting. My talk was on "Pawnee
...pic" - I just read the paper grandad
...ote up describing the magic tricks
...ncle Lute had seen. Every one thinks
...+ should be published! In an anthropology
...magazine! We may take a week off, soon, to
make our furniture. gosh - we're so slow
getting started + the house nearly done
Saw Mr. B. in Coolidge - he was at the
Conf. - and he'll be up soon.
Much love, + many thanks
Courtney

About the Author

Courtney Reeder Jones grew up in Lincoln, Nebraska. She has traveled widely and has lived in the Southwest, Puerto Rico, and the U.S. Virgin Islands. She studied architecture, anthropology, and archaeology at the University of Nebraska and the University of Arizona. In addition to her experience in the National Park Service, Jones has worked as a dressmaker, freelance writer, and museum curator. Her current project is the publication of her annotated "Kitchen Diary" from 1938, her first year at Wupatki. Since 1956, she has lived in Santa Fe, New Mexico, where she continues her lifelong involvement in politics and community organizing. Jones is an avid reader and likes to walk along the Santa Fe River.

About the Editor

Lisa Rappoport spent four years working with horses in western Europe before studying philosophy at Trinity College, Dublin. She is a graduate of St. John's College in Santa Fe, New Mexico. In addition to writing, editing, and photography, her occupations have included construction work, housepainting, and gardening. Rappoport's photographs have been shown in New Mexico, New York, and California. Her poetry has been published in several journals, and she is working on a collection of short stories. Her current editing project is an oral narrative of the Everglades for a book by noted photographer Mary Peck. Rappoport now lives in Oakland, California.